Energy Management
Mantras for Caregivers

By

Mamta Mishra

Energy Management Mantras for Caregivers

By Mamta Mishra

Fifth Estate Publishers, Blountsville, AL 35031.

First Printing, 2025

Printed on acid-free paper

ISBN 13: 978-1-958450-17-8

Fifth Estate Publishing

Fifth Estate, 2025

Noteworthy Reviews

A Beacon of Empowerment: Mamta Mishra's "Energy Management" – Fueling Change for Neurodiversity. Mishra, a true force for good in the global autistic community, infuses the same dedication and insightful understanding that has marked her activism. Mishra's work in advocating for autistic communities globally is nothing short of transformation.

The endorsement of Marcus Boyd, a renowned autism global activist, further underscores the significance of "Energy Management." Boyd's encouragement for others to read this book speaks volumes. His recognition highlights the book's potential to be a genuine catalyst for positive change, offering valuable insights..."Energy Management" is more than just a self-help guide; it's a testament to Mamta Mishra's unwavering commitment to creating a more equitable and understanding world...It's a book that has the potential to empower individuals, shift perspectives, and ultimately fuel real and lasting change. For anyone asking a fresh and compassionate approach to personal energy management, and those dedicated to fostering neurodiversity, this book is an essential read.

-Marcus L. Boyd, a renowned global Autism Activist, humanitarian, music producer & composer, and Lifetime Presidential award winner.

There are three main goals in writing a book aimed at helping others.
You must establish common language and terms.
You must have advice that is applicable to the situation.
You must present it in an accessible and memorable format.
*In her book, **Energy Management Mantras for Caregivers**, Mamta Mishra not only achieves but excels in all of these.*
One of the most difficult things for caregivers to do is to care for themselves in the midst of demands.

Mamta Mishra clearly lays out and explains how to use coping skills, how to manage your internal resources and energy, and how to keep from drowning in the internal and external clutter constant demand can generate. Beginning with advice on coping and how to structure your environment to advice on navigating the internal blows of criticism and problems of aging, this book is a manual for all caregivers, regardless of the condition or pathology of those in their charge.

Dr. Joseph Lumpkin, Dr. of Ministry, Masters in Divinity, Author of Three Best Selling Books - The Books of Enoch: The Angels, The Watchers, and The Nephilim..., The Lost Books of the Bible: The Great Rejected Texts, and The Book of Giants.

Energy Management Mantras for Caregivers by Mamta Mishra
The author has done a remarkable job of telling the interesting true-life story of her efforts in managing her second son Parag's Autism who was diagnosed when he was two years and
seven months. She is a natural storyteller who gained the skill from her ancestors who were storytellers.
True to her name "Mamta" which means mother's love, with her commitment and devotion to her son, she was able to help him manage his symptoms and use his potential to make gel candles and Ayurvedic cosmetics. She wisely recognized the crucial importance of taking care of herself: managing her own energy to prevent burnout and performing well. She shares that wisdom through this book...She has explained the word "Mantra" in the title as a tool to think. A lot of people are aware of the word mantra from its use in many meditation practices.
The cover of the book with a painting by Parag is beautiful and meaningful. A great many stories in the book from various sources are seeds of wisdom for the readers. This is a very informative, insightful and inspiring book.
N. S. Xavier, M.D. Psychiatrist and Author of *The Two Faces of Religion: A Psychiatrist's View*

Energy Management: Mantras for Caregivers by Mamta Mishra is a thoughtful and empowering guide for long term caregiving, which demands extraordinary physical and psychological fortitude from the caregivers. Mishra gives examples from her own experiences of taking care of her autistic son, Parag, who is now a self.-taught artist. She draws from deep insight and compassion to offer strategies that help caregivers not just survive but truly sustain their energy and emotional well-being over the long haul.

*At its core, this book recognizes that caregiving, especially for those supporting individuals with complex needs, requires more than patience- it demands endurance, resilience, and intentional self-care. Mishra provides readers with **practical lifestyle** changes aimed at restoring depleted energy, such as adopting healthier routines, prioritizing rest, and creating realistic boundaries.*

*While the book is rich with helpful tips, readers looking for more clinical advice or structured behavioral strategies may find this guide more focused on personal well-being than on child-specific interventions (unlike her first book, "Autism, Our Journey and Finding Happiness). However, this emphasis on **self-restoration** is exactly what makes it a vital resource for long-term caregiving success.*

Overall, Energy Management: Mantras for Caregivers is a must-read for parents, teachers, therapists, and support workers seeking sustainable ways to manage their caregiving journey with compassion, endurance, and hope.

Highly recommended *for anyone who needs a reminder that caring for others begins with caring for oneself.*

G. Michael Shehi, Sr. M.D., M.A.,
American Board of Psychiatry and Neurology

Assistant Clinical Professor of Psychiatry, Edward Via School of Osteopathic Medicine
Medical Director and Owner, Mountain View Hospital, Gadsden, AL

Tribute

This book, "Energy Management Mantras for Caregivers," is a tribute to my dad, Mr. B. N. Jha (February 18th, 1940, to January 1st, 2024). He was a scholar who lived an exemplary life. He held a degree in social welfare, philosophy, law, and business management. He worked as a director personnel in Steel Authority of India Limited for 23 years and then served Engineers India Limited as a chairman/director personnel until his retirement in 1998. After that, he taught Business Management to executives. Teaching was his true passion, and his professional career came to a full circle, for he had started his career as a professor of philosophy at Ranchi University, India.

He was the founding father, a visionary, who, as the town administrator, helped develop Bokaro Steel City as one of the first planned cities in India, and he helped recruit 30,000 people in Bokaro Steel Plant, the first indigenous steel plant of India.

I am blessed to be his daughter, who has benefited from his philosophy of working for the greater good. Every time he counseled and advised me with his wisdom and experience, I said, "If I become 1% like you, then I will be able to do so much good!" He always laughed when I said this. Well, this book, *"Energy Management Mantras for Caregivers,"* is my attempt to do the 1% of good in memory of my dad, whom I miss and love!

Dedication

I dedicate this book to all the people who have been behind the scenes supporting and encouraging me to sail through my life and deal with Parag's Autism with love, courage, and hope! I believe anyone's story of success is the product of the cumulative help and encouragement of people behind the scenes. My life is a **story of progress,** and the journey continues, so it is not a story of success. Success is the final destination. Lines from Robert Frost's poem "Stopping by Woods on Snowy Evening" resonate with me: **The woods are lovely, dark, and deep, But I have promises to keep, And miles to go before I sleep, And miles to go before I sleep.**

First and foremost, I dedicate this book to caregivers who take care of their loved ones day in and day out without much respite. Their dedication is inspirational. They redefine love! I also dedicate this book to my elder son Ankur; he has been a silent pillar of support! He has been present like an iceberg; only ten percent is visible, and ninety percent is submerged in his effort to help everyone. He steps aside so that his brother, Parag, can capture the limelight.

My husband, Pranav, is my "rock of Gibraltar." He has been my anchor in life, a safe harbor. I am thankful to my parents, grandparents, my siblings, Kamna and Ajay, who have actively supported me and been there during the darkest moments of my life! I am thankful to Dr. Anthony Metcalfe for making time to edit this book. I am thankful to all my friends who have made this journey fun; they are the oasis of my life. To all of you, I say namaste: I bow to the divine in you!

About the cover art:

This book cover is one of Parag's paintings. Parag has autism and no formal education in painting. When COVID-19 hit in 2020, his vocational training in making candles and ayurvedic cosmetics came to a standstill because the two places that supported him and sold his products closed for a while.

To keep him engaged meaningfully, I gave him canvases to paint on. Through self-guided learning, he started enjoying the process and creating spectacular artwork. It is beyond my imagination to see him develop techniques like layering, stamping, and mixing colors to express what he had already created in his mind on the canvas.

When painting this flame, he put yellow paint at the bottom, then blue, and to his astonishment, the paint turned green. He stepped back and observed the change of color with wonder, figuring out that when yellow and blue mix, it changes to green. He decided that he liked the way color had changed. Parag used glitter paint in the flame's white portion, giving it an ethereal glow.

Table of Contents

SECTION ONE:

Mental Energy States!

"Energy is liberated matter. Matter is energy waiting to happen."

— Bill Bryson,

Preface

Let's understand the title of this book: **Energy Management Mantras for Caregivers.**

According to the dictionary, energy is defined as **"capacity for doing work." Management is "the process of dealing with." Mantra** comes from the Sanskrit root words "man," **to think,** and "tra," **a tool. A mantra is a tool to think! "A caregiver is someone who is responsible for taking care of another person."**

This book is a sincere effort to help caregivers find tools of positive thinking to optimize our physical energy by realigning it with mental, emotional, and spiritual energy, enabling us to perform to our full potential with satisfaction and happiness.

I believe there is a tremendous need to start a candid conversation on this topic. This topic resonates with everyone because we all are caregivers. We have an innate need to give the best care to our loved ones. However, long-term caregiving for loved ones with chronic disease, disorder, or ageing with illness takes a huge physical and psychological toll on us. According to "Caregivers Statistics: Portrait of Family Caregiving in 2023", the number of unpaid family members in the U.S.A. is 53 million. The National Institute of Health published an article in 2022, "caregivers' burden and its prevalence measurement scale." According to this article, 31.3% of caregivers felt distressed, 24.7% experienced an increased social burden, 26.7% had disturbed routines, and 30.9% felt high financial burden. Therefore, managing personal energy is critical to giving high-quality care to our loved ones.

My son Parag was diagnosed with autism when he was two years and seven months of age. Dealing with Parag's autism is a very challenging feat that demands constant vigilance, planning, and patience! Believe me, when one has a kid with autism, the probability of days not going the caregiver's way is always high. Anyone dealing with caregiving for a chronic illness or disorder is always uncertain how their day will go. These coping skills, which are the tools, techniques, and mindset that I am sharing in this book, equip me every day, but they are even more handy in dealing with my bad days or the days that are not going my way. I was a control freak, and Parag's autism taught me that nothing is in my control. I had to learn how to develop coping skills to manage my day. These coping skills have helped me survive the day-to-day tsunami of unpredictability in my life.

We all know that when we take care of ourselves, we become better at caregiving, but we don't know how to take care of ourselves, and when we make time for ourselves, we are laden with guilt because we perceive that making time for ourselves is selfish. We know that when we fly in an airplane, we are warned that in case of emergency, we should put the oxygen mask on ourselves first and then help others. However, in life, there are no physical masks falling in our laps to save us so that we can save our loved ones. These coping skills are the virtual masks that come to our assistance in times of need.

Energy Management Mantras for Caregivers is a recipe book of coping skills for physical, mental, emotional, and spiritual wellbeing. After reading the book, we can reread a chapter according to our emotional needs. Just like when we want to cook a dish, we go to the page where the recipe for that dish is written. For example, when we feel rejected, then we can re-read the chapter "Mental Decluttering: Shedding Guilt and Rejection," or when we feel like a loser, a failure, the chapter "Healing and Growing from Failure" will let us reevaluate and reenergize us to pick ourselves back. When we feel the dearth of love from a loved one, reading the chapter "Love is Multifaceted" helps us understand this abstract concept with concrete examples. This chapter helps us understand and separate love from romance. Thus, building a relationship with much needed clarity and fortification. The chapter "Mental Decluttering: Shedding Anger" enlightens us that anger is normal and there is no shame in it; it is a release of a pent-up energy in the form of anger. Learning to release that pent-up energy so that it is not destructive but rather constructive is crucial to self-development and growth. Every chapter stands on its own, for it is a part of the whole! Once we internalize these coping skills, we can combine them in various combinations and permutations to help ourselves when life throws a curve ball at us.

My ancestors were tremendous storytellers, and, in this book, I have shared some of the stories that I heard from my great aunt, grandmother, and my dad. They told me stories that teleported me to a world of fantasy and immense imagination. Some stories were from Ramayana, Mahabharata, and Panchatantra. All these stories had morals, and protagonists never gave up or gave in to facing their challenges. Later in life, I realized that stories divert our mind from our immediate situation to soothe us and give us courage and hope! As a child, these were just stories that were fascinating and entertaining, but later, they became my anchor because I realized these stories have deeper meaning and life lessons. These stories became my oars to sail through the turbulent waters of life, and I hope they give you solace, respite, and energy as well.

Gradually, I started telling those stories to my siblings and cousins, they loved to listen. I enjoyed their mesmerized looks and exclamatory sighs as they listened. To make my stories more interesting, I would modulate my voice depending on the situation or the character. Later, this voice modulation helped me in teaching Parag and in regulating his behavior. It is a powerful tool in the field of behavioral science.

 Soon after, I started making up stories and would stop at a critical point. They would beg me to tell them more, eagerly waiting for the story to end. I, too, did not know how the story was going to end, for it was cooking in my head organically. The beauty was that "good guys," heroes, in spite of their hardships and challenges, remained steadfast to their thoughts, words, and actions. Therefore, they won, and the "bad guys," or villains, were dishonest in these three essential qualities therefore they lost in the end. After all, all of the stories I had listened to were about good winning over evil. The reality is life can be more complex and convoluted, but we all want "good" to win, and that makes us human beings "being human"!

I want to share a real-life incident that happened. After Parag's diagnosis, I was going to India to get help from my parents and siblings. My elder son Ankur started getting fidgety in the airplane, so I started making up a story for him. After about an hour or so, I asked him to go to sleep, and he started saying, "Mom, please more," and the guy who was sitting behind us said, "Please more!" I looked back and felt so embarrassed that he was listening to my story all the while. He said that he was enjoying my story and that he would like to know how the story ends. Now, I remember this incident with a smile, but at that time, I felt so mortified. In hindsight, I realize that words are powerful, and they can bring people together!

I did not know that the universe was preparing me to tell my story through dealing with Parag's autism and that it was molding me to become a real-life storyteller. As I tell my story, I get the opportunity to listen to the stories, and experiences of my readers and audience in my talks. These stories are powerful connections that bring us together in the journey of life.

People ask me all the time, **"How do you have so much patience? Are you always this put together?"** Whenever I get this question, in my head I think if only they knew the truth! **All these questions can be collectively summed up to: How do you maintain patience, energy, enthusiasm, happiness, and fortitude despite the daily grind of dealing with Parag's autism?**

This question does not have a short and simple answer and answering this in-depth meant telling the story by opening the flood gates of physical, mental, emotional, and spiritual dam and then letting you see how I have harnessed energy in the form of coping skills from the turmoil and chaos that Parag, my younger son's diagnosis of autism brought in our lives.

Until now, I have deflected answering this question in depth and detail by telling them that the answer to this question is in "Chapter 3: Parag's Diagnosis and My Cleansing" of my book *Autism Our Journey and Finding Happiness*. This is a pivotal chapter for me because, if the cleansing of all the negativities that were holding me back had not happened, then I would not have written any of my books. Before I could develop these coping skills, I had to go through a process of cleansing and decluttering the physical and mental space, which started the path of emotional healing. I found out that getting rid of these negativities is not a one-time deal, but it is an ongoing process. Just the way we do a spring cleaning of our physical space, our mental space also requires intermittent cleaning.

I had not planned to answer this question elaborately because answering it has resulted in the daunting task of writing this book and adding one more task to my plate. I am a multi-tasking mama; some days I wish I had eight hands like goddess Durga, so I could perform all the tasks at the same time. Writing this book or, for that matter, my first book, *Autism Our Journey to Finding Happiness,* was not on my bucket list. **I believe one thing leads to another because we are meant to learn lessons from these incidences and interactions, and nothing changes till we do.**

What Propelled Me to Write This Book?

Both books are the results of organic incidents. The following incident propelled me to write my first book, *Autism Our Journey and Finding Happiness*: I went to a flower shop in Gadsden, and when I gave my credit card to the lady who was helping me, she looked at the card and said, "Are you the candle maker's mom?" Oh my God, I was elated for she recognized me with my son, Parag's ability. Parag makes gel candles and ayurvedic cosmetics, and in Covid, we accidentally found out that he is a gifted painter. When I came home, I took out a notebook and, standing by the kitchen counter, started writing the book. When I lifted my head up, two and a half hours had passed by, and the first manuscript of my book was done. After that, all the good stuff happened: the editing, re-editing, and then, with God's grace, I found a publisher who published the book. Once the book came about, people started sending friend requests on my personal Facebook page, so I made a public Facebook page with the same name as my book and started answering people's queries on autism. This has created a community of 134,000 followers. Through this Facebook Page, I share Parag's trials and triumphs. His progress has been slow but steady due to consistent and persistent efforts. This gives hope to so many to go on with their challenges. It is great to find my "Tribe" and not feel lost and lonely in the journey of life.

This book, "Energy Management Mantras for Caregivers," happened because I counseled a student who was studying to be a special education teacher. She follows my Facebook page, and she is a very responsible young lady. She has a sibling with severe autism and a mother who takes care of him 24/7. The outbreak of Covid had stalled her plans to graduate and that was making her extremely anxious and hopeless. I redirected her thoughts and said that the most important thing for her was to be safe for life is the most precious gift that Universal All-Pervasive Energy has bestowed on us. She would be able to help out, provided she understands that being alive and healthy gives her this opportunity to serve her family and the community. Of course, the large part of the counseling is listening and letting it pour out; it is like draining the pus out of the wound, and once that happens, the wound heals, which leads to emotional well-being.

The style of writing in this book is a stream of consciousness, compilation of thoughts, feelings, memories, stories, and anecdotes that showered on me like meteorites. It has not been easy to go back in time to inspect, organize, and compile the journey of caregiving and share these coping skills that I have developed over the course of twenty-five years. I hope and pray that these coping skills become tools for your health, healing, and happiness as they have been for me!

Why Did I Develop These Coping Skills?

Parag was diagnosed with autism when he was two years and seven months of age. I had not even heard the word autism before. The more I read and researched, the more depressed and disheartened I would become, because there is no cure for autism. However, I did not want to believe that. I thought that if I took him to all the speech therapy and occupational therapy and did everything that is out there for autism, he would be all right.

It is humanly impossible to do everything that is out there for autism because when you type in "autism" in the Google search bar, 531 million results pop up in 44 seconds. The more I read, the more confused I became. During this phase of my life, I was like a rudderless boat drifting away in the tsunami of information. Moreover, people were giving me tons and tons of advice for Parag's treatment, and I was trying to incorporate all of them. Later in life, I realized that people are free with their advice, even when they really don't understand the predicament. Social media makes everyone think that they are an expert by just imbibing a two-minute clip on something that could be total fiction, but it is accepted and imparted with conviction. Some of the advice was downright ridiculous, and it made me sad and angry. One person told me that I should do nothing and accept Parag the way he is because if God wanted him to be normal, then he would have sent him thus. I thought accepting doesn't mean doing nothing. When the neurotypical baby comes to this world, we equip him or her with knowledge and values to live a life of highest potential. Why should it be different for a neurodivergent kid? Trying to assimilate all the information meant more and more work for me, and I became a headless chicken, going round and round in a circle. What a dissipation of energy!

I became so scattered during this phase of my life that it is not even funny. This excerpt from my book *Autism Our Journey and Finding Happiness,* chapter 3: Parag's Diagnosis and My Cleansing, Page 15, reveals my state of mind:

> "I worked with Parag like a person gone crazy. All the anger, frustration, and rejection made me snappy, hardheaded, and blind. Also, my obsession with healing Parag did not let me rest. I was mentally and physically exhausted. All this negativity started manifesting itself physically; I was absent-minded and zombie-like. Even when I was not teaching Parag, I was still thinking and making plans for his improvements.

These incidents will describe my chaotic state of mind. One day, Ankur, my older son, was late for his swim practice. I was trying to get everything together and rush out with both my sons. Ankur looked at me and said, "Mom, you don't have a shirt on." Another time, I sat in a car that belonged to someone else, thinking it to be mine. The seat did not feel right and that made me realize my blunder. I also remember punching a phone number in the microwave. My husband happened to see this and jokingly said, "Come back, our children are too young, you cannot go crazy right now." His words had some magic. I believe that made me really come back and reevaluate my life."

During this time, I also developed perpetual back pain, and when I went to the doctor, he said, "Mamta, can you carry a 50-pound potato bag?" I said, "Of course not!" Then he said, "Stop carrying Parag around. That is giving you this back pain. Take care of yourself." I couldn't tell him that it was so much easier to scoop Parag in my arms and escape the glaring eyes of people when he was having meltdowns and tantrums. Those who deal with the autism of their loved ones know that our days are filled with unpredictable manifestations like those. Therefore, developing coping skills for us caregivers and for the kid with autism is a game changer.

Then something amazing happened that changed the course of my life. One day, someone gave me one more piece of advice: I should teach Parag in a room where the walls are painted white with nothing on the walls and a white sheet on the desk. According to his research, they learn the best in a sterile environment; I broke down, and I had reached my elasticity point. "I called Parag's pediatrician, and to this day, I believe that God spoke to me through him. He said, "Mamta, autism is not like a fever that goes away after a while. Autism is a disorder for life, so you need to change your mindset." He said, "Whatever is not good for Ankur is not good for Parag. For example, too much sugar is not good for Ankur, and that is true for Parag too. **To deal with autism, the best course of action is to make your household as normal as possible.**" (*Autism Our Journey and Finding Happiness*, Chapter: Advice from a Pediatrician, Page 21)

I went on thinking about how I could make my household as normal as possible, and then one day, in a meditative mood, the answer came to me: **"simplify!"** At that very moment, I chucked away all the alternative medicine that I was giving to Parag: vitamin C, vitamin D, B12, fish oil, a Secretin hormone, and gluten-free diet even though he is not allergic to gluten. Then, Parag had to eat whatever I was cooking for the rest of the family, and it simplified my life! It took away the workload of preparing special meals and made my household somewhat normal. Kids with autism are already picky eaters, and by preparing specialized meals, I was limiting his choices even more. Parag is now a foodie, and I have shared how he metamorphosed into an epicurean in the article "How to make kids with Autism Eat Healthy and Hearty" on my Facebook page *"Autism Our Journey and Finding Happiness."*

After this, I decided to gather all the ammunition of evidence-based knowledge I could find. I went to Jacksonville State University to get my master's in special education, and that gave me direction in helping Parag. That is when the journey to move forward started, and the journey continues!

Why is Personal Energy Management Not Working?

Before we discuss the title of this chapter, we need to ask ourselves, **why do we need to manage personal energy? Energy is the fuel to think and to perform!** The quality of our daily lives is dependent on our energy level. Energy and enthusiasm go hand in hand. Optimization of energy helps us allocate it to better health- physical, mental, emotional, and spiritual. **To live a happy and fulfilling life, managing personal energy is an absolute must!**

We make to-do lists, schedules, and timetables. With the timetable in place, we begin a race with time to complete the tasks, and to deliver, we start burning the midnight oil. This means lack of sleep and leads to anxiety and stress. It feels like time is winning, and no matter what is ahead of us, we are exhausted! **Why is this not working?** It is not working because we are trying to manage the wrong thing: **Time. When we manage energy, time automatically falls into place.** It is pointless to compete with time because time is infinite, and we have been given finite time on Mother Earth. So, when we pace with time, we end up with an energy deficit.

To manage that energy deficit and not get exhausted. We start drinking coffee, which gives us caffeine high, and sugary food, which gives us sugar high. We start performing, but it is temporary because this "sugar spike" that enables us to push our performance is accompanied by a "sugar crash." To balance off the extra sugar in our blood, more insulin is secreted to compensate for the sugar spike, and then we cannot pick ourselves up due to energy deficit. When we drink booze, it has a different effect than caffeine and sugar; it makes us feel that the problem is gone, and then when we wake up, we not only have a headache, a hangover, but the problem is still there and now even more looming. These are temporary rebooting or quick fixes to the CPU, the central processing unit, our brain. Our brain is the most magnificent biological computer ever created. Our brain does not like these quick fixes. We start showing hardware failure, that is, our body starts manifesting diseases because of this recurrent abuse to our body through these quick fixes. Due to this undue stress, we start having health issues like depression, anxiety, heart problems, diabetes, immune system disorders, etc.

So, the analogy that comes to my mind is that these quick fixes are like driving the car on a doughnut. We know that we cannot drive our car on a doughnut for a long distance, and if we do, then accidents are bound to happen. These quick fixes are like doughnuts, and we cannot solve the long-term energy deficit with these quick fixes.

So, the important question is, how can we fix our personal energy depletion? The answer is that we can fix energy depletion by making lifestyle adjustments and developing coping skills!

Three Mental Energy States

Buddha said, "We are what we think!" Descartes said, "I think therefore I am." So, thinking is very important because we become what we think! The brain just goes on generating random thoughts through the five senses: sight, sound, smell, hearing, taste, and touch. The mind tries to organize this massive input of information into feelings and emotions. According to the laboratory of Neuroimaging at the University of Southern California, the average person has about 48.6 thoughts per minute. That cumulates 70,000 thoughts per day. This is an unconscious phenomenon. We are not even aware of what we are thinking. When we catch a thought or react to one, then that thought gets converted into emotions. It is an active process. The word emotion has been derived from the Latin word "emotere," which means energy in motion. Indeed, emotions are a state of mind that is never static. **We reach the state of emotional well-being when we demonstrate unity, no discrepancy, between what we think, what we say, and what we do! This means we are honest with ourselves at three levels: thoughts, speech, and deed!** It is important to have high quality thoughts because it is the raw material that gets converted into high quality emotions! Our thoughts can make us stay in one of the three mental energy states. They are:

First, a high positive mental energy state. In this mental energy state, we are hopeful, passionate, enthusiastic, and optimistic with fully focused energy, which leads to the highest level of performance because we are highly motivated. **In this mental energy state, we experience joy.**

Second, a low positive mental energy state. In this mental energy state, we go on performing well because we experience **happiness**, which is the aftermath of experiencing joy. We experience all the qualities and attributes of the high positive mental energy state, just toned down because we are still reminiscing and experiencing being in a state of joy. The example that comes to my mind is the birth of a baby, that instant is nothing short of miracle and a joyful moment. I suppose that is why we call a baby a "bundle of joy." Then when we show off the baby to friends and family, we are happy because the memory of that miraculous moment plays in our head.

We should renew and recharge to go back to the high positive mental energy state, and perform to our highest potential again, and experience joy again. Our goal should be to recharge and catapult ourselves to a high positive mental energy state. This enables us to oscillate between experiencing joy and happiness!

The third mental energy state is the negative mental energy state. In this mental state we are hopeless, burned out, indecisive. We experience **extreme sadness**. It is critical to avoid this mental energy state. All of us have experienced this negative emotional state at one time or another. It could be due to the loss of a loved one or due to diseases and disorders that we face ourselves or through our near and dear. It is due to a challenging situation or a traumatic experience that life throws our way. **It is of utmost importance to avoid the negative mental energy state at all costs.**

I say this because I have been there and lived there; it is a dark vortex of negativity. After Parag, my son's diagnosis of autism, and finding out that it has no cure, I spiraled into this dark bottomless pit, with the speed of lightning. I got buried in the tsunami of hopelessness and sadness. It was a Herculean effort to dig myself out of that desolate space. When we are spiraling down that bottomless pit, we are continuously looking down and don't see where we are going to land. It is scary and transfixes us, petrifies us. All we need to do in that freefall state is to tell ourselves, "I am not going to fall," and in that very moment, the hypnosis of that fall is broken because in that moment, we choose courage over sadness!

When we understand that life is tough for everyone, we don't squander away this precious gift in living in a negative mental energy state. I love cooking, and those of you who cook know that when we buy meat that happens to be tough, we don't throw it away, but we put tenderizer in to make it soft. In the same way, we have to soften our lives with the tenderizer of kindness, love, empathy, and friendship. These are very important qualities that allow us to grow our emotional quotient and live a high-quality life of happiness and fulfillment.

You may ask, why can't we be in a state of joy all the time? Only Buddha or an enlightened human being can be in a constant high positive mental energy state of joy all the time because they are like Noble gases. Noble gases have eight electrons in their outermost orbit. This means they have a full octet, which makes them stable; that is, they do not react easily, which makes them "Noble!" Just like noble gas, the enlightened human being or Buddha has a heart full of **love and wisdom** that makes them stable, and they, too, do not react easily but remain in a state of contentment, joy, and bliss.

We mere mortals react all the time because we react to people and situations all the time. So, what do we do? We have to learn from electrons. Electrons gather photons (light energy), and then they go to a higher orbit, the higher energy state. Once they spend that energy, they come back to their original orbit, the lower energy state, to gather photons or energy and go back to the higher energy state again. We, too, like electrons, need to oscillate between a high mental energy state of joy and a low positive mental energy state of happiness. **What are our photons? Our energy! Our photons, or our energy, is positive thinking!**

How to Be Happy

The "happiness pie" (after Lyubomirsky et al. 2005, p. 116). Original caption: "Three primary factors influencing the chronic happiness level"

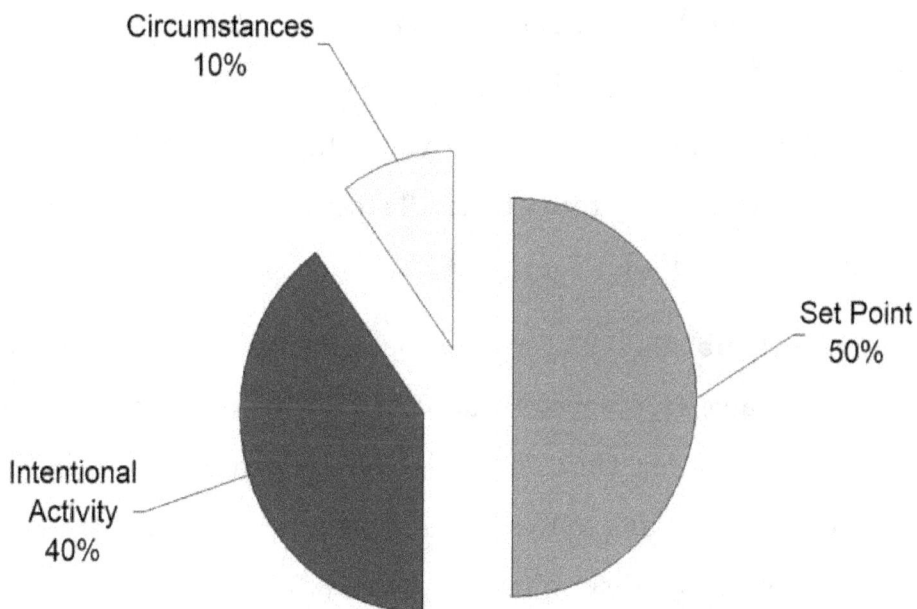

Circumstances 10%

Set Point 50%

Intentional Activity 40%

How Can We Think Positively and Be Happy?

What is happiness? Happiness is being alive in the moment with a thankful heart and purposeful mind! Why do we want to be happy? According to the research, happier people are more productive. They have better social lives, relationships, resilience, good health, and long life. Well, the simple answer is it feels good to be happy! **How do we know we are happy?** When we are happy, we exude energy and enthusiasm. We feel, "I've got this!" This doesn't mean that it is easy to deal with challenges, but we are choosing to be ready to handle them with fortitude and a positive attitude.

Sonja Lyubomirsky et al 2005 published an article, "The Sustainable Happiness Model and Pie Chart: A Heuristic Framework for Understanding the Influences on Well-Being." According to this article, researchers said that 50% of happiness is determined by genetics, 10% is determined by your circumstances (finances, health, living situation), and 40% is contingent on your own intentional efforts to become happy!

So, the gist of this research is that even though genetics and life circumstances are significant variables for happiness, we can teach ourselves to be happy with intentional activities and behavioral interventions. Now, it is very important to understand that this 50% genetic predisposition to be happy or not be happy doesn't get expressed automatically. Just because one has a predisposition to cancer does not mean they will have cancer; it just means that given certain conditions or circumstances, they have a greater likelihood that the cancer will manifest. In the context of happiness, too, people who are genetically predisposed to get sad and depressed have a greater likelihood of being unhappy, but lifestyle choices and environmental modification play a huge role in the gene not expressing itself!

When we go through extreme unhappiness because of life's circumstances- death, disease, disorder, etc.- then we not only appreciate and cherish happy moments, but we learn to create those and try to live in this mental state of contentment and cheer.

Happiness is a skill, a learned behavior. That means that with repeated practice of positive thought and proactive behaviors, we can be happy. Elbert Hubbard, a famous American writer and philosopher, said, **"Happiness is a habit- Cultivate it."** We may not have read his books, but we often quote his words: "When life gives you lemons, make lemonade."

To be energetic, enthusiastic, and happy, we have to learn to develop a metacognitive skill, which is defined as **"thinking about thinking!" That means what we do with all that thinking.** We all think, but when we become aware of what we are thinking, it allows us to analyze why we are thinking certain thoughts and how to channel these thoughts into a positive outcome! This stage of metacognitive thinking is "reflective thinking," a huge self-awareness tool in our arsenal, and this is the point when our knowledge and experiences start culminating into wisdom. To reflect on thinking is a learned behavior and by no means automatic. Thinking is largely an unconscious process, but doing something with the thinking process is very much a conscious process!

Before we can think positively, we need to be aware of what we are thinking. That is what thoughts we are catching, like fish from the ocean of the unconscious mind, and examining. This examination is Metacognition. This awareness of our thinking helps us change and regulate our emotions.

Once we can be in tune with what we are thinking, we can figure out ways and means to slow down the process of repetitive thinking or overthinking. We already discussed in the chapter "Three Mental Energy States" that we process

70,000 thoughts per day. We tend to think the same thing aimlessly and repeatedly without any resolution. According to the National Science Foundation, **95 %, or 66,500,** of our thoughts are repetitive, and **80%**, or **56,000,** are negative. We think positively only **20%** of the time in a day, and that amounts to **14,000** positive thoughts. The loop of repetitive and negative thoughts dominates the thinking process and drags us to the negative mental energy state that I have stated, and we should avoid this state.

We have to slow down thinking before we can train our brain to think positively and keep us in the two high mental energy states of joy and happiness. Why do we need to slow down our thinking process? Well, we want to give the ever-active and overactive brain, our magnificent biological computer, some rest so that it can recharge and reboot to function better. Nature's gift, to slow down thinking, is **sleeping**. Scientists believe that **we never stop thinking,** but when we sleep, the process of thinking slows down, and it is proven that we heal the most when we sleep. When we sleep, the brain's filing system works better, it reorganizes, consolidates, and integrates the information that it collects throughout the day into our memory so that we can retrieve it and recall it when we need it. When we sleep well, we are able to work with renewed focus and enjoy our day better!

The next step is to detach ourselves from negative thinking. How can we do that? To detach from anything, we have to attach something else! In behavioral science, I have learned to replace undesirable behaviors with desirable behaviors. For example, when Parag was little, he got upset and bit his wrist, a self-inflicted behavior (SIB) that many kids with autism show. As a coping skill, I put a wristband on his wrist and gave him a hanky to bite on when he was frustrated. He always has a hanky with him, and he has learned to bite on it when he is flustered. This is a transference or replacement of an undesirable behavior into a desirable behavior.

Through teaching Parag, I became aware that we can replace undesirable thinking with desirable thinking. We have to be conscious of our mental energy state, and once we know we are becoming off-centered because of the building up of negative thoughts, then we can break that cycle by choosing to do an activity that absorbs us or engrosses us completely.

When I start slipping into negative thinking, I consciously transfer my negative thoughts with actions that completely absorb me. I do gardening or cooking, and it helps me; it calms me down. It is therapeutic. The action distracts and diverts my negative thinking by thinking about the task at hand. The end result of these activities is very gratifying because my garden bears tremendous harvest, and my cooking became an epicurean delight for family and friends. These activities, gardening and cooking, distracted me from negative thinking. Sharing the fruit of labor with family and friends brings me happiness. In my talks, I say that when I start thinking negative and energy-dissipative thoughts, I start singing the line from Frozen, "Let it go, let it go!" My audience laughs, but I am dead serious. This is an immediate response to shed a negative mental energy state.

We can stop negative thinking by developing a mental flip switch! My grandma was brilliant in instilling positive thinking. She flipped an incident that we may perceive as negative into a positive one. For example, while eating, if any of the family members accidentally toppled a glass full of water, she would immediately say that spilling water is a good omen, for it means that the ancestors were thirsty, and this quenched their thirst. In case of an accident, she would immediately say, "Thank God, it could have been worse." If my grades were not good, she would say, "Thank God you did not fail; next time, you will do better." Recently, I was warming a bowl of vegetables for Parag in the microwave, and it burned my fingers and fell from my hands. My first reaction was to thank God and say that it was not so bad and that Parag did not get burnt. At that moment, I realized that I was using my grandma's mental flip switch to think positively.

I plan my day. I make a schedule. It is a habit that rarely does my day go as planned, but this does not dip me into a negative mental energy state. When I was younger, things not going the way I had planned would irritate me, upset me, and dip me into a negative mental energy space of beating myself mentally for my inefficiency. Thoughts like *I am a loser* triggered the parrot that was sleeping in my head. Once it woke up, it started saying tons of negative things. Until my energy dissipated, I was in a depressed mood. It made me feel that I had failed, and that was my destiny. It is very easy for a mom of a special needs child to think she is a failure. Not only have others said that about us, but we too tend to think like that ourselves.

However, now that I am consciously harnessing the power of the mental flip switch, the moment these thoughts harangue my mind, I switch it on. Thanks to my grandma and my great aunt, they said, "When our plan is failing, then God's plan is taking over, and that is always the best plan!"

As John Milton wrote in *Paradise Lost*, "The mind is its own place, and in itself, can make a heaven of hell, a hell of heaven."

How can we think happy? A long time back, I read a story that has stayed with me, and it answers this question. The story goes like this: some scientists performed a social experiment to test the temperament or thought process. They selected two toddlers for their experiment. They put the toddlers in a room with a huge pile of horse dung. One kid started crying and wailing the moment he was left alone in that room. The second kid started digging through the dung fervently. When asked why he was digging though the horse dung, the kid said, "if there is so much of horse shit then horse is buried under this, and I have to save him." **To be happy we must find reasons to be hopeful, even when we are surrounded by challenges that stink like shit.**

My husband often says I live in LaLa Land. This mental space, what he calls LaLa Land, is a happy mental abode, an oasis. I wish my Lala Land was a real place because this utopia would change every gun into a flower! For that sanctuary is a place of **love**. My mental oasis helps me to handle challenges and hardships. I know I can go back there to recharge and reset. This mental escape to happy thoughts has made me deal with my challenges with replenishable energy. After seeing the movie Pollyanna with Parag, I, too, started finding reasons to be happy! **Counting our blessings and living in gratitude is a great practice for being happy! Optimism and pessimism lie in our attitude and how we see the glass. Is the glass half empty or half full?**".

What works for me apart from exercising negative thoughts with absorbing activities like cooking, gardening, and exercising? Finding a quiet place, my yogic spot, mostly in nature because Mother Nature helps calm me, gives me time to meditate in solitude and recharge. My mother lives in India and, in times of stress, I want to put my head in her lap and feel her soothing hands on my head, gently brushing away my worries and negative thoughts. That is not possible in my day-to-day life, for I live in the U.S.A., and she is in India. So, I turned to Mother Nature for help. She is gentle and nurturing, like my mother.

Sometimes, we hold unnecessary thoughts in our heads for so long that they gnaw at us, and it is a considerable dissipation of energy. The easiest remedy is to talk about it with the person who can answer the question that is eating us up. The story I read about the two monks illustrates this negative mental state very well. The two monks were about to cross a flooded river. A woman asked the monks to help her cross the river. One monk said they couldn't help her because their oath to celibacy forbids them to touch a woman. However, the second monk asked the woman to get on his back, and he swam to the other side of the river, got her safely down, and then bade her goodbye. Both the monks continued their journey to their monastery. Once they reached the monastery, the first monk told the second monk, "You were not supposed to touch a woman, and you carried her on your back!" The first monk said, "I put her down at the riverbank yesterday, but you are still carrying her in your head." This story lets us know that we carry an unnecessary burden of thoughts, to the point that it festers our minds like parasites. This is a huge dissipation of energy!

One time, a friend asked me, "Are you really happy, or do you pretend? I just looked at her, laughed, and I said, "I practice thinking happy!" She looked at me quizzically. Life always throws curve balls at us, and we all dip into sadness. I too still do, but I come out of that funk pretty fast because *thinking* happy has made me a **"hopelessly hopeful"** person.

Before you start reading the next section of this book, I want you to pause, reflect on what we have read, assimilate the relevant information, and evaluate it for your own energy management needs!

First, Mental Energy State:

> **High Positive Mental Energy State-** In this state we are hopeful, passionate, enthusiastic, and optimistic, with fully focused energy. This leads to the highest level of performance because we are highly motivated. In this mental energy state, we experience **joy!**
>
> **If you are in this state all the time, then this book is not for you. You are the master of personal energy management!**

Second, Mental Energy State:

> **Low Positive Mental Energy State-** In this energy state, we experience all the above qualities of the first energy state, but toned down, so we experience **happiness** in this state. **If you are in this state, that means you experience joy sometimes and sadness sometimes (mostly you are happy). This book is for you because it will give you tips, hands-on applications and coping skills to improve upon your mental energy state and reduce experiencing sadness so you can be in the mental energy space of happiness and joy even more!**

Third, Mental Energy State:

Negative Mental Energy State- In this mental Energy state, we are hopeless, burned out, and indecisive. We experience **extreme sadness.**

If you are mostly sad, that is, most of the days you feel stuck with no forward movement and end up coming back to the energy state of sadness, then this book is definitely for you!

Let's ask ourselves:

1. What information mentioned in this section will enhance my energy and happiness?

2. How am I managing my personal energy?

3. Which Mental Energy state I am often in?

4. What can I do to oscillate between the two positive mental energy states?

5. What are the things I can do to be more energetic and happier?
   - Relaxing and sleeping well
   - Replacement of thoughts with higher quality ones
   - Activating mental flip switch
   - Talking to the person who can resolve the issue
   - Practicing an attitude of gratitude

6. How can I develop my own coping skills for my needs?

SECTION TWO:

Decluttering and Shedding

Negativities

"Clutter is not just the stuff on your floor – it's anything that stands between you and the life you want to be living."

Peter Walsh

Decluttering and Shedding

Trees are the greatest gurus to teach us to shed and rejuvenate. The tree sheds dry limbs, leaves, and flowers because this enables new growth. Trees always preserve what is integral to their existence and growth: the root and the trunk. Similarly, we need to shed old ideas and belief systems, and in doing so, we find new stuff, new ideas, new people, and new space to grow into the best version of ourselves! Just like trees, we, too, need to preserve and protect ideas, values, beliefs, and people that are integral to our existence and growth. They are our roots and trunk.

Clutter means excess stuff that is disorganized and haphazard. The clearing of space or decluttering of stuff and thoughts increases our "capacity to do work," that is, it increases our energy and productivity. The second law of thermodynamics states that the universe is naturally inclined to gradual disorder or entropy. To fight entropy, clutter, or disorder, we have to work, that is, put energy into decluttering and organizing. This is not a one-time deal, but we have to declutter again and again because clutter tends to perpetuate itself. We cannot declutter the entire physical or mental space in one go; it should be gradual, just like the trees. Trees don't shed all the leaves in one go at the onset of Fall. We should choose what we want to declutter.

Decluttering the physical space is easier because we see the clutter. Even then, it is a "Mission Impossible" to declutter the entire physical space in one go.

In many countries and cultures, we have a season allotted for deep cleaning, which is decluttering and reorganizing. For example, in the USA, we have a specific time for "spring cleaning," where we make time to get rid of what does not serve. In India, we don't do spring cleaning, but we clean our physical space during Diwali, the festival of lights. We do this to invite Goddess Lakshmi, the goddess of wealth and prosperity, to our homes. The thought behind this is that decluttering leads to an unobstructed flow of "panchmahabhutas "the energy flow through the five elements with which the universe is made: earth, water, air, fire, and sky. Thus, this decluttering of physical space enhances energy flow and promotes mental clarity and harmonious surroundings for improvement, learning, and growth.

In this materialistic world, living with excess is a habit. There is a constant bombardment of advertisements that entice us to buy more, which compels us to collect things and hoard. We are tremendous hoarders of things and thoughts that don't serve us and that makes it very hard to make our physical or mental state clutter free and tidy. I, too, have collected clothes, shoes, and other accessories over the years. When I was younger, I would try to organize my closet and all I did was rearrange the clutter. Even the things that I would take out to discard, I would go back to check if there was something that I still needed to keep, and believe it or not, almost everything went back on the shelf. The thought behind this hoarding was that I may not need it now, but in the future, I may have a need for this stuff. **Rearranging the clutter is not a solution. Discarding what is not needed is necessary for personal growth.**

Mental decluttering is harder than physical decluttering because we do not see this clutter. We feel it due to our emotional responses to recurrent thoughts that keep us captive in the negative mental energy state. To tidy this space is much harder because, over the years, these thoughts are jumbled together, and separating these clumped-up thoughts is like separating a tangled wool ball.

I remember my mom would ask me to take out the wool yarn from an old sweater. It was a tedious task, and sometimes the wool became intricately tangled. Untangling the knots of the intricate maze of tangled wool and gradually making an organized ball was a work of disciplined patience. Once the ball was done, my mom could make a new sweater with a new design. Similarly, some thoughts are like knots; we have to untangle those thoughts, one at a time, so we can organize them, cut off the portion that is too tangled, and join the yarn together with the most seamless knot. That is how we reuse the yarn to make a new beautiful pattern.

How do we know which thoughts to declutter first? The thoughts that drain our energy the most need to be addressed first. When we recurrently think the same thing, it is important to figure out which part is the most bothersome and debilitating. Once we know that, it is a huge accomplishment because it means we succeeded in untangling the hardest emotional knot. This is awareness, a conscious effort of acknowledgment; this is when the journey of moving forward begins.

However, even when we do the process of untangling thoughts, we never complete it, and that is why, many times, we heal to some extent but not completely. We tend to catch the thought that weighs us down and sometimes even talk about it, but we fail to act, or we may take an action and stop midway. Therefore, the loop for emotional well-being never gets completed. After thinking and saying, the third requirement of emotional well-being is acting! The ball of yarn that we untangle will not knit itself into a sweater. The action of knitting is required to make a new sweater. Not taking action or acting not to the completion is like not knitting the sweater or knitting it halfway. So, the beautiful pattern never emerges or emerges halfway.

When we forgive ourselves, we also forgive others because we learn to let go of what is not serving us. This clears up the mental space for growth. **How do we know that we are on the path of emotional recovery and well-being?** The recurrent debilitating thoughts don't play on our mind's screen, and if they sometimes pop up, then they don't make us uncentered emotionally. We know to replace this thought with a positive one by activating the "mental flip switch" that we discussed in the "How Can We Think Positive and Be Happy" chapter.

A few years back, someone told me that once she moves on, she doesn't look back. There is a difference between moving on and moving forward. When we move on, we resign ourselves to our situation and people without completely healing, and we still move with a lot of mental clutter or baggage. We don't want to look back or look within because we are scared of opening up wounds that were never healed. I say this because looking back, I see my personal journey of mental evolution and healing. Let me share a paragraph of my first book, *Autism Our Journey and*

Finding Happiness, chapter 3, Parag's Diagnosis and My Cleansing. Ten years have passed since it was published in November of 2015. In the book, I wrote, "I promised that all the dark negative thoughts will be nailed and boxed, and this Pandora's Box will never be opened and peeked into for it will bring nothing but negative energy and misery. "To err is human," and I have sometimes gone back and peeked into this box, and it brought me nothing but pain. So as time has passed, I have become more determined and hopefully smarter because I don't peek anymore. I am able to warn myself."

This is exactly what this person was telling me in her own way, and I understood because I have been at that place of mental evolution, and the above paragraph is the proof. However, now I also understand that her journey of decluttering and healing is not complete. Many of us stop evolving at this point because we have decluttered enough to not feel stuck, there is a movement, and we don't want to delve deeper into our consciousness. The hardest ones hide in the deepest depth. To examine these, we have to forgive ourselves completely, which is not an easy thing to do because we are weighed down by guilt, hurt, pain, anger, sadness, and so forth. However, when we have the epiphany that the mistakes that we make in life are like accidents because they, too, are not desired or designed, we forgive ourselves, and we know that we will not repeat these mistakes. This is learning and a solemn oath to ourselves. This allows us to move forward.

When we move forward, we travel light because we have truly decluttered and healed. The people who move forward are warriors, and they wear the scar as a reminder of their bravery. They are not scared of looking back because when they look back, they are happy to see how far they have come along on this journey of life. So, now looking back and opening the "Pandora's box" is not scary for me because I know that it is actually my **treasure box** of memories, experiences, knowledge, and wisdom.

Decluttering adds quality to life. It is a catalyst for improvement and growth. Once we declutter our physical and mental space, we allow an unobstructed flow of energy. It increases the quality of our lives, which is the harbinger of happiness! Decluttering or shedding negative emotions is a subjective process. Everyone goes through their own challenges, and they have to summon courage to declutter or shed the negative emotions that are hindering them from growing emotionally and spiritually. In the following chapters, I am writing about some of the emotional clutter that I had to shed so that I could heal and grow again! I hope you can relate and find these coping skills valuable in your own healing, happiness, and personal energy management.

Mental Decluttering:
Shedding Guilt and Rejection

Guilt and fear of rejection are very debilitating emotions. Human beings are social animals, and we want to be accepted and included. We want to fit in with our friends, family, and colleagues. Not being able to fit, or being different, gives us the fear of rejection and being ostracized.

To my surprise, I witnessed the stigma and taboo associated with an autism diagnosis in the United States of America, one of the most developed countries in the world. I have come across many parents who fear their kids getting the diagnosis of autism, even though they know that their kid is showing all the symptomatic behaviors. They believe this "label" will direct negative societal attention toward their kid. India is my birth country. There is a stigma attached to special needs in the Indian community. It is deeply rooted and slowly changing through education and awareness. When I was growing up, I heard many people call a special needs individual not by their names but by their disabilities. For example, they called the blind person "aandhe," which means "blind man," or a lame person "langre," which means "lame man."

What is ironic is that two gods in my culture are special needs, yet they are the most powerful Gods: Ganesh, the God with Elephant head, and Hanuman, the God half human and half monkey! Ganesh blesses with knowledge and wisdom and brings good luck, taking away obstacles. Every auspicious occasion starts with seeking blessings from Ganesh. Hanuman bestows strength, courage, and power to surmount any challenge or hardship in life.

The fear of rejection makes family members hide special needs kids from their kith and kin. This is how they protect their kids and themselves from social rejection. The worst thing is that the individuals with special needs themselves think that God has cursed them for their bad karma in their last birth or births because that is what they hear from people around them all the time! This becomes their **"illusionary truth!"** This is a psychological phenomenon where we hear lies repeatedly and recurrently, and we start perceiving them as true. That is why we have a saying, "When we hear a lie 100 times, we believe it." The treatment of society instills undue guilt in neurodivergent individuals and their families. This is debilitating because it makes them feel flawed. The guilt builds into shame. The shame of being different and not able to fit in with the norm takes a huge toll on special needs individuals and their families.

Absolving oneself from this undue burden of guilt is not easy!

After Parag's diagnosis, I had to face comments that Parag was born to me because of my sins from my last birth or births. "Only one thing a woman can do right is give birth to a normal child, and you could not even do that." This is just one of many examples of what I was going through. Rejection and emotional trauma created by the actions and words of people were very tormenting. My initial reaction was anger somewhat like what Timon advises Simba in Lion King: "When the world turns its back on you, you turn your back on the world" (*Autism Our Journey and Finding Happiness*, Chapter-Parag's Diagnosis and My Cleansing, Page 15). All the guilt and rejection was hurting me and making me extremely sad.

Guilt comes from the feeling of doing wrong, and it generates regret. I believe no mother plans to give birth to a special needs child. The day I realized that Parag is a blessing from God and God never makes mistakes, that is the day when what people said stopped bothering me. My sons, Ankur and Parag, are my greatest blessings from God. My name is Mamta, which means mother's love, and I wear this name as a crown, for this is the best role I play in my life. All the other roles that I play are different hats!

When we are different, and fear of rejection overpowers our thinking, we choose to isolate ourselves. The International Board of Credentialing and Continuing Education Standards (IBCCES) conducted a survey, and according to them, **87%** of families with special needs never go on a family vacation, and one of the reasons is fear of rejection. We are worried not only about how we will manage when we leave home but also about what others will think about us and our situation. We think this way to protect our loved ones and ourselves and to avoid rejection or the unpredictability of stepping out from home with a special needs loved one. One thing this fear of rejection definitely does is make us recluses. It is easier to not go out at all than to mingle with people and be a part of the community.

One of the deficit areas in autism is the lack of social skills. Not giving kids with autism the opportunity to interact with people hinders their ability to learn this skill set. Pranav and I decided not to hide Parag but to share him with people who understood that being different is not being less. This was not an easy decision at that time because Parag's tantrums and meltdowns were a constant in our daily lives. This decision worked for us because we did not become socially isolated, and over time, Parag has become a social butterfly and a party animal. He is very gregarious.

What I have found out is that when we share our situation with people, most everyone is accommodating and understanding and ready to work with us. In 2007, we took Parag with us on a family vacation to Italy. On the first day of arrival in Rome, the tour guide had organized a meeting with all the tourists who had booked the same tour. We shared with them that Parag has autism. The entire group adopted Parag with love and care. Only Parag had the privilege of eating on the bus. All the people on the bus realized that Parag loves to eat barbeque-flavored chips. They started treating him to chips, and Parag expressed his thanks with hugs and smiles. Being included makes us happy, and this is true for everyone. "Parag is happy because he is an active participating member in the family. Parag doesn't feel left out as a family member and is able to go everywhere with us, to restaurants, movies, games, and vacations. The biggest part of inclusion is that we talk to him, and he responds back." (*Autism Our Journey and Finding Happiness,* Chapter-Why is Parag happy and what has worked for us? Page 192)

These days the social media platform plays a huge role in people feeling rejected and the reason is that they think this platform is for true friendship, but that is not so. It is a very superficial interaction that lacks the emotional connection that nurtures a friendship. I see people, not just kids, getting heartbroken when their so-called friend blocks them on social media. This ghosting has led to psychological problems of rejection, "otherization", guilt, and depression.

There was a point in my life when some so-called friends stopped talking to me. It hurt me, and I tried to find the reason for secluding me. I never got a reason from them for this rejection. Talking never happened. After a painful introspection, the hurt gave me a profound understanding that it was time to find my flock. I understood that we were different tribes because my tribe would never abandon me. **Finding our tribe is important to be happy.** It is fulfilling to find a common purpose for improvement, camaraderie, and growth! When we find our tribe, we resonate with synergy, which is a great experience because it is the amplification of cumulative energy from each member of the tribe for a common goal. In doing so, we learn to uplift each other and chip into each other's well-being and happiness.

In finding supporters and believers for autism spectrum disorder, I experience this feeling of belonging and purpose. By starting the Autism Foundation of Gadsen AL,

I have found friends/comrades who have come together with all their hearts and souls to spread autism awareness and acceptance for the individuals with autism. What a joy it is to spread hope and happiness together!

We know that nature rejects us when we do not have the ability to adapt to changes. Darwin's theory of **"survival of the fittest"** means that in the evolution process, we must adapt to not get rejected by nature. **Adapting helps us to not just survive but thrive because instead of fearing rejection, we embrace change with the sense of adventure and positivity in this journey of life!**

The Paradox of choice!

Learning to choose is hard. Learning to choose well is harder. And learning to choose well in a world of unlimited possibilities is harder still, perhaps too hard.

Barry Schwartz, in his book *The Paradox of Choice*

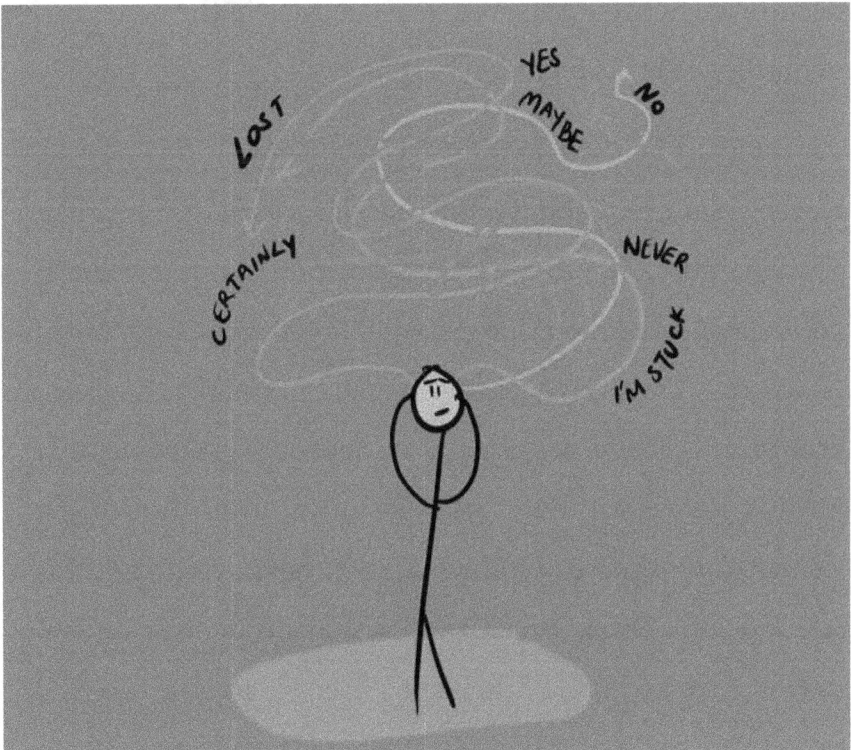

Mental Decluttering: Shedding Confusion

Shedding confusion is the first step towards thinking coherently and not being scattered by dissipative thoughts. Shedding confusion requires sorting, categorizing, and compartmentalizing our thoughts so that we can decide and act. However, in this "new media age," we have boundless choices and information at our fingertips to empower us, and yet we are lost and confused. We think and rethink, but we are scared to make a decision because that might mean we do not get to experience the immense choices that are out there. The fear of not making the right decision or not being the best one keeps us in the doldrums of inaction. This is mental paralysis.

I wanted to help Parag, but I did not know how. I was reading all I could about autism, and it was very confusing. The Internet is flooded with information about autism. If you type in autism on Google 531, 000,000 results pop up in 44 seconds. The problem is that not all information is correct and useful. There are articles and people believing that MMR vaccines are the cause of autism, even though the Center for Disease Control (CDC) has debunked this scientifically. Many organizations and groups for autism firmly believe in the Chelation Theory. It is a medical procedure that uses chemicals to remove heavy metals from the bodies of children with autism. Some believe certain foods cause autism, like gluten and dairy. There was an article I read, which was published by The Royal Society of Medicine in 2015, which believes that circumcision in boys leads to a high risk of autism. Later, this research was debunked as well. After reading so many viewpoints, with so many approaches, I was utterly confused. I was like a rudderless boat, lost in the tsunami of information on autism.

A few months after Parag's diagnosis, I went to India with my sons, Ankur and Parag, to visit my parents. One day, I asked my father for advice. My dad worked in the prestigious position of director of personnel in Engineer's India Limited. As a head of the human resource (HR) department, his job demanded people management for the company. He dedicated his life to problem solving for the company, motivating the employees so that the firm could grow and everyone working for the firm grew with it! I am one of many people who have always looked up to him for guidance and inspiration. **I asked him, "How am I going to live my life? My life ahead feels gloomy, and I am so confused".**

He looked at me deeply, intently, and with a smile, he said, **"No confusion, no learning."** He said that searching for an answer begins with confusion! Confusion is the desire to seek knowledge and answer to the predicament. He said that I should learn a life lesson from the women who carry pitchers of water on their heads. The pitcher is on their head while they animatedly talk, joke, and laugh. He explained that even though these women are enjoying themselves, their focus is the pitcher, and that is why it does not fall and break. He said that Parag's autism should not stop me from enjoying my life, but I should always be focused on my goal, and that is to take care of Parag with love and patience! My dad said that seeing Parag happy would give me the energy to move forward with my duties and responsibilities and fulfill various roles as a mother, wife, daughter-in-law, friend, author, speaker, etc. I am so thankful for this advice because it not only helped me gather myself but also gave me direction to not live my life as a recluse. It is very easy for a caregiver who has to deal with a chronic health issue or lifelong disorders of a loved one to do so. This advice gave me "the zeal to deal with autism with all the gusto and positive energy and to compartmentalize my life where there is space for being alive and happy!" (*Autism Our Journey and Finding Happiness*, chapter Parag's diagnosis and my cleansing). After experiencing the paradox of choices in the world of autism, I came out of this funk and brain fog by deciding to hold on to evidence-based education in the field of autism.

So, from my experience, I know that when we are confused, seeking help from the right person, who can guide us and prod us in the right direction is tremendously helpful. In this information age, freedom comes with setting our own boundaries. Boundaries are when we actively choose *this is what I want, and this is how much I want*. Setting our own parameters to choices and information gives us clarity, connectivity, and control over our own lives.

Mental Decluttering: Shedding Fear

Fears are perceptions of threats because we don't feel safe. Perception of threats can be real or imagined. Both real and imagined fears dissipate our energy and happiness. Fear keeps us in a state of inertia and inactivity; fear freezes us. More often than not, the fears that we face in life are not external but internal. I have not met a person who has been chased by a beast because that is a rare occurrence. We are often devoured by the beast that is internal, and fear is one of those beasts. To fight a fear that holds us captive and keeps us in a state of inertia, we need external force to shake it off.

 Inertia is Newton's first law of motion. In layman's terms, objects will be in the state of rest or constant motion until or unless they encounter external force. For example, to move a desk, we need to apply an external force of pushing or pulling. Otherwise, the desk will be in a state of rest forever. In the context of shedding fear, the external force is **"practical solutions!"**

To deal with the fears, real or imagined, practical, common-sense solutions are necessary. The following anecdote proves the point. One man was not able to sleep at night because he thought that there were monsters under his bed.

He went to the therapist, who asked him to look under the bed, and that would take away this fear once he realized that there is nothing under the bed. However, he could not summon courage to peek under his bed. One day, he told his best friend about his predicament. The friend said, "I have a solution." He sawed the leg off the bed and told his friend, "If you had come to me in the very beginning, you would not have spent an atrocious amount of money on the therapist!" We all need friends to have our backs and a bond to share our deepest fears; that is the best therapy.

Well-wishers and true friends are the external force that jerks us out from fear that grips us into the state of inertia. In 1995, I had a car accident, and I developed a fear of driving. Pranav, my dear husband, cajoled me to sit behind the steering wheels. At that moment, I was upset at him, but looking back, I am so thankful for making me do so and helping me get rid of that fear.

Ankur, my elder son, learned to swim very well when he was little, but he wouldn't go to the deep end. He had the fear of drowning. My brother, who was teaching both Ankur and Parag to swim, tried to logic it out with Ankur that the whole point of learning to swim is to not drown, but Ankur did not want to take that risk of swimming in the deep end of the pool. The fear of drowning gripped him.

One day, my brother let go of Ankur from his arms into the deep end of the pool. Ankur swam back to the shallow end, and from then on, he not only got rid of the fear of drowning, but he became one of the best swimmers in the swim team.

Many times, we don't do something because our brain perceives that action as risky, and that generates fear in our minds. We are hesitant and fearful because when taking risks, we have to leave our comfort zone, the space of safety. When we take risks, we may fail, and sometimes, the thought of failure creates inertia. I have dedicated a chapter to "Learning from Failure." When we think of failure as an opportunity to learn and grow, we don't fear it, but it becomes a challenge that we want to pursue; it becomes a quest to find a new horizon, an adventure. We take risks in so many things throughout the day, but we do not think about it because our mind has processed that fear to the point that it does not perceive it as a threat. I can give many examples, but this one is the one we don't even consider a risk: when we eat, we can choke to death, but our mind perceives it as not a likely event. Therefore, we not only eat, but we enjoy it thoroughly. Calculated risk helps us take action and get rid of fears that hold us incapacitated and inactive. Calculated risks are strategies and plans to convince our minds to take the leap of faith and overcome fear. Michael Jordan said, "You miss 100% of the shots you don't take."

This means that when we don't take a chance for the challenges and predicaments we face, then we lose without even trying. Not trying is being in the state of inertia, a passive state of acceptance of the predicament. Calculated risk is the external force, an active process to change the outcome of a situation. To take calculated risks is a determination to rise above the fears with a concrete plan and predictions through the process of critical thinking and problem solving and then working diligently towards the desired goal.

The fear of unpredictability of the future grips the caregivers who are taking care of loved ones with chronic disorders or diseases. The National Institute of Health (NIH) published an article in 2022, **Caregiver burden and its prevalence measurement scales.** According to this article, 31.3% of caregivers felt distressed and fearful of the future outcome. This happens to many caregivers because there is no immediate solution to the predicament we are facing. We dwell on these questions, which have no concrete answers in the present, and then we start thinking about dreary future scenarios, and that is a huge energy dissipator that makes us anxious. To deal with them, we have to apply the strategy that works for the standardized test. We are taught to tackle the easier questions that we know we can solve and then address the ones that are really difficult because it will take more time to solve or answer. If we don't adhere to this advice, then the chances are we lose points because we are stuck trying to solve a difficult problem, and in doing so, we lose time, and we end up not answering the questions that we could have answered easily. **We lose time because we dissipate energy.** Making the most of the time is conserving energy for the best results.

Caregivers dread the thought of not being around for their loved ones. I, too, have a daunting question: What will happen to Parag when we are not around? Pranav, my husband, and I are still figuring out how to make the best plan for Parag's future so that when we are not around, he is taken care of. The plan is evolving as he is growing, and we don't have concrete answers yet. It gives us solace and encouragement to look back because we witness that he has come a long way. As the journey of his progress continues, we see he is requiring less assistance, and he is becoming independent in taking care of his daily needs. I hope and pray for the right solution. I am hopeful that there will be some remarkable research in the field of autism, and we will find a cure. Hope is a great propeller and buster of fear! I pray for this miracle, and that gives me solace, peace, and energy to move forward.

The above question has no concrete solution right now, and if I go on focusing my energy to solve this, then I will lose time, energy, and happiness. So, I focused on a fear that I knew was solvable. The fear of losing Parag in a crowded place was so gripping that I used to have recurrent nightmares. They have subsided because of the coping skills that I developed. However, these fears are like dormant volcanoes, and they may surface with anxiety building up.

The fear of losing Parag in a crowded place had its roots in the fact that when Parag was little, he used to shoot like an arrow. He is still limited in expressing himself verbally. We came up with a behavioral intervention to stop his tendency toward elopement.

"Parag used to shoot away like an arrow. He did not have a fear of being lost in public places. We had to be so careful when we took him outside. One time, we were in the mall, and before we knew it, he had taken off towards the water fountain. I did not want him to get lost, so it was important to train him to be with family. In India, my siblings and I took Parag to the park, and we would all walk side by side with him. After a few days, we all decided to hide behind the trees and shrubs and see what Parag did. He went on walking for a bit, but once he realized no one was with him, he stopped, looked around, and then just stood there looking for us. We came out, and he looked relieved to see us. We were very happy to see this reaction because this was the first time he had shown emotion or hesitation and did not walk away without caring. We also taught him to hold hands in crowded places. In 2006, we took him to see the Christmas tree at Rockefeller Center in New York. He clutched my hand so tightly. The fear of getting lost was in him. Now, he keeps an eye on family members and likes to keep everyone together! When we go out to movies, restaurants, and games, he likes to round us up and make sure that we are all leaving together. There have been times I have forgotten my purse or sunglasses in the restaurant, but Parag does not forget. He retrieves them for me. So, the fear of getting lost not only made him keep the family together but he also gained a keen sense of awareness for our material possessions"

(Autism Our Journey and Finding Happiness, Chapter: Early Intervention, Page 48).

Later on, I came to know that dealing with elopement tendencies in kids with autism is a huge challenge for caregivers. Other practical precautions that we have taken are that Parag has an ID wristband stating that he has Autism and the address and contact phone numbers of caregivers. Moreover, we have taught him to say and write his name, address, and home phone number. When he steps out of the house, he puts the air tag in his pocket; that way, we can track him from our phone.

Fears are subjective, so coming up with a plan to intervene comes largely from common sense, which I believe is the most uncommon thing and most required thing to live a happy life! We cannot overcome all our fears in one go. Decluttering fear is like cleaning dirty laundry; we cannot overload the dirty laundry in the washing machine because that will not do the job of getting the clothes clean, and the machine may break down. To clean the clothes, we have to sort them by color, and then we decide which ones need to go in the washer first. In the same way, we have to sort, prioritize, and figure out which fears we are going to tackle first. **Maya Angelou's lines make perfect sense when dealing with fears and other predicaments: "Do the best** you can until you know better. Then when you know better, do better."

Mental Decluttering: Shedding Anger

Charlie Chaplin said, "We no longer need to fear arguments, confrontations, or any kind of problems with ourselves or others. Even stars collide, and out of their crashing, new worlds are born. Today, I know "THAT IS LIFE!" Anger, like many emotions, is part of being human. Anger is triggered by the sympathetic nervous system as a "fight or flight" response to the situation that we perceive as a threat. **Anger prepares us for a fight**. It is a natural feeling, and there is no shame in knowing that we are angry. It is a manifestation of our discontent, which is a culmination of multiple negative thoughts: shame, guilt, fear, hurt, etc.

We are mere mortals. Even God gets angry. Every culture has a story of God's anger and forgiveness. The story of God's anger that stuck with me from my childhood is one about the most powerful God, Shiv. Shiv wanted to see Parvati, his wife, but Ganesh was guarding the bathroom while his mom was bathing. She had instructed him not to let anyone come in. Ganesh stopped Shiv from entering the bathroom. Shiv got angry and chopped Ganesh's head. What a terrible story. Now, this is a story of Gods, so its ending is not as tragic. When Parvati came to know of this tragedy, she begged Shiv to bring her son back to life. Shiv put a baby elephant head on Ganesh, and he was alive again. I feel that even though Ganesh came back to life, the consequence of his dad's anger was carrying the heavy elephant head forever.

Before we can learn how to release anger without damage, we must know what makes us angry and what triggers it. Why are we angry? When Parag was diagnosed with autism at two years and seven months of age, his diagnosis shattered everyone! My family is highly educated. The grandparents were dismayed and heartbroken to know that Parag may not go to college. Everyone was hurting and licking their own wounds. No one was empathetic to others' emotions, for everyone thought their own hurt was the biggest and most painful. The environment in the house was just acrimony. The one person who was hurting the most was my son, Ankur. He is just ten months older than Parag, and he was not able to comprehend this chaos around him. My husband, who is a physician, said, "There is no cure for Autism!" I saw the pain in his eyes and heard the hurt in his voice. This man cures so many people every day, and he could not cure his own son. I was not able to feel his pain then because my pain was blinding. I was angry, hurt, full of guilt, and lost! We all were so focused on our pain that we were trying to lick our own wounds instead of putting healing balm on each other!

The fact that autism has no cure was worse than a death sentence. The extreme hopelessness of the situation made me extremely sad and depressed. This was not fair; I wanted a cure that was not available. A state of utter helplessness made me bitter, which is an amalgamation of sadness and anger. Not knowing what to do and where to seek help made me angry. I wanted friends and family to try to understand without being didactic. Without wearing the same shoes, people tend to be free with advice, what to do, and how to do it. Now it amuses me, but when Parag was diagnosed, it made me angry. Their advice was mainly something that I was supposed to do, and I was already stretched to the point of mental breakdown!

The fact that Ankur, my elder son, and Parag could not grow up like normal siblings made me angry. The fact that Parag was not included in the birthday parties made me angry. I was hurting, and I couldn't communicate, and that manifested in anger. My circumstance made me angry, and at that time, I did not know how to release anger appropriately. **My anger stemmed from the fact that I was searching for solutions and trying to understand the** situations and the reactions of friends, family, and my own.

I got so hurt and angry by many incidents, but two incidents shaped my thinking at that time, and it helped me to redirect my thoughts and gain understanding. I realized that people say things not necessarily to hurt but out of ignorance, uncouth behavior, and a habit of saying things. A high school kid with a big heart offered to play with Parag for an hour or two while I could tend to other responsibilities. At a gathering, her mother shared that while her daughter was jumping on the trampoline with Parag, his poop went flying everywhere from his diaper. I was there listening to this exaggerated statement, for Parag had pooped in his diaper, and I cleaned him too. There was no flying poop here and there and everywhere. She was relating the story as a funny incident, and people at the table were amused by it too. I cringed inside and thought that Parag was five years old and nonverbal, so helpless, and people were already making fun of his disability. I came back home and cried helplessly, which was a release of all the pent-up emotions. **I promised myself to speak up for Parag and protect him. Sometimes, the release of that anger not only has a cathartic effect but helps us make constructive decisions about the predicament we are facing. The outcome of this incident was that it became a**

catalyst into making me Parag's advocate and helped me become an avid advocate for Autism awareness.

The second incident happened when I was taking special education classes at the university. One of the projects that I was assigned was to record a half an hour of a teaching session with a special education student and get feedback from a layman. I gave a recording of my teaching session with Parag to a friend to watch and give me written feedback in a paragraph or two. After two weeks, when I inquired, she had not made time to watch the video clip. She promised me that she would do so soon. However, she did not make the time. A few hours before my presentation, I went to collect the video clip and the feedback, but to my dismay, she had not made time. I was shocked when she handed me the video clip and apologized for not making time. I was so shocked and upset that I was dumbfounded. I cried and drove all the way to school. When my turn came to present my video, I told my classmate and the professor that the person to whom I had given the video clip could not make time. I also had to analyze the given feedback, whether I agreed or not and if not why. I said it was apparent to me that people who don't deal with a similar situation do not want to make time to understand the challenges that do not concern them. I later realized that the above statement is not true; there are people who want to understand and help because they are kind and loving.

I ended my presentation by cracking a joke. I said that, now that this has happened, the professor will give a zero on this project. Everyone laughed. In the dark moments, my ability to find humor and crack jokes about it has been a gift from God. A sense of humor helps us not to dip into the "negative mental energy state." After this incident, **I promised myself that I would choose my friends wisely!** I believe that challenging times make us understand the phrase "a friend in need is a friend indeed." **The experiences that make us angry sometimes have life lessons embedded in them!**

"During this time, I took another trip to India with my sons to visit my parents in order to find respite and solace. I told my dad all the stuff I was feeling and that I was so angry at myself and everyone around me. He told me a story, and it changed my thinking. Now I know that anger is a false strength and that understanding and compassion are the real strengths. I wanted to embrace these qualities, but I found out I could not get them, and I had to cultivate them in my heart. With time, I learned that sometimes people say and do things because they do not understand and act out of ignorance. All I had to do was accept this fact just as I was accepting Parag's autism. **Acceptance gave me the courage to move forward.** I also understood that no one can hurt us until we give them the power to do so. My dad told me a story that helped me understand this, and I want to share this wisdom. The story was that when Buddha was preaching, someone started bad-mouthing him. Buddha's disciples got upset and were surprised to see that Buddha was not affected by the profanity directed towards him. They asked him how he could be calm. Buddha replied, "He is giving, but I am not taking." Through this story, I learned the important difference between listening and hearing. I listen, an active process to the words I value and cherish, and hear, a passive process to words I forget *(Autism Our Journey and Finding Happiness, Chapter 3- Parag's Diagnosis and My Cleansing, Page-14)."*

In that moment I understood that we give power to others to hurt us and make us angry. Through this story, I also learned to differentiate between listening and hearing. Listening is an active process of recognizing words that are valuable and worth remembering. Hearing is a passive process to words that can be dismissed.

I asked myself why I was listening to everyone and wearing myself out. The answer that came to me was that I believed everyone to be my well-wisher and that they may know the answer. I was twenty-three when I got married and came to the United States. I was young and naive and did not expect harm from anyone. The reason for this thinking was I was raised by a loving and protective family who wished me well without fail, and when I needed help, they helped me. It was a lesson for me to figure out who my well-wishers are and choose to listen to them. This self-analysis made me realize that I am my biggest well-wisher. Also, as a mother, I am my sons' biggest well-wisher. My name is **Mamta,** which means mother's love! Life has tested the meaning of my name; it was given to me by my parents, but now I know I have earned this name!

Learning to release anger without damage! Dams lead to the proper release of excess water from the rivers, and they avert death and destruction in the same way the channelized release of anger is a must to avoid hurting others and ourselves. When anger is released in a channeled manner, it makes us feel better, lighter, and happier. The proper release brings solace, peace, understanding, and deeper bonding.

Anger tends to make the receiving person angry at some point as well. Any object, when it meets a heated object, will gradually become heated as well. Anger is a transfer of heated words or actions. It rubs until the other party displays anger too. Just like puss needs to come out of the wound to heal the body, anger needs to be released for our emotional healing.

If you have used a pressure cooker for cooking, then you know that it is essential for the excess steam to come out; otherwise, the pressure cooker will burst. Our brain too becomes the pressure cooker, and when excess frustrations, pent-up thoughts and feelings, unfulfilled expectations and desires that are not let out simmer, then we burst either with verbal outburst or, in extreme cases, physical lashing out. Anger never manifests out of blue, just like there is no rain without clouds, the same way there is a valid reason for the display of anger, going to the root cause of that outburst is the awareness that leads to healing and stopping the hurt. Learning the proper release is a must. We all know that "a stitch in time saves nine."

There are times when anger can manifest in physical lashing out, and I have counseled some families to figure out coping solutions with appropriate release and alternate solutions. For example, instead of wanting to hit a person, redirect that need on a punching bag or a pillow, or go shoot ball in the basket. This is the transference of negative thoughts with an activity that helps release them without any damage to people and things around us. When we are aware of the buildup of the mental negative energy state and find a physical, quiet space, we inculcate the ability to detach from the trigger and calm down. Sometimes venting to a sympathetic ear, who can be a sounding board, works and helps us gather ourselves because listening to what we think makes us put the pros and cons into perspective and figure out an amicable solution. Sometimes, seeking professional help is the best course of action.

Many times, kids with autism show self-inflicted behaviors, that is, they injure themselves by hitting, pinching, or biting themselves. This is their way of expressing ple*ase listen to me, help me, I am here*. Once I started **talking** to Parag, my relationship, both as a mother and teacher, became so much better. Our time together in school became so much more productive, and the learning and teaching process became both amicable and pleasurable.

Talking is crucial in averting anger, and that pent-up energy is released in a peaceful manner. Peace treaties between countries are examples of finding a solution to collective mass anger. Talking happens when we are honest with our thoughts, words, and actions to ourselves and to others. In counseling for autism, before I can talk, I have to listen intently. **Listening and responding are very**

important aspects of talking. Reacting is anything but talking! Sometimes we worry, and just by talking to an empathatic friend or family member, we find an alternative perspective. We all know that "two heads are better than one," yet we try not to take that help. Taking the right help at the right time from the right people helps us not to be unbalanced and lose the equilibrium of mental peace. **Every human being wants to be seen, heard, respected, and loved.**

There are times when it is not the energy field of another person but my own that is unbalanced and leads to anger or frustrations. That state of analyzing **why I am feeling this way and what will help me** have been critical questions, and knowing those has been vital in finding my emotional balance before it starts to discharge. For example, the moment I start becoming snappy, I catch myself and try to analyze the reason. Most of the time, it is overwork and over-commitment. The analysis helps me to take some rest to feel better.

I realized that to take care of Parag without getting flustered and angry was to find **the right help**. One of the reasons for my frustration and anger was that I was overworked and did not have the right help to move forward in life with fortitude. Let me explain what I mean by "right help" with an analogy. If you want yogurt and I give you cheese, it doesn't help you, even though both are made from milk. So, it is very important that help is a solution to the required need. A headache cannot be cured by medicine for stomach viruses. Going to college to get my master's degree in special education was one of the best decisions I made because it gave me tools and means to tackle Parag's autism with evidence-based knowledge and not get lost in the jungle of information on autism. Starting Parag's homeschool and teaching him where he is happy and productive gives me the energy and enthusiasm to go on.

Without teamwork, I could not have succeeded in running Parag's homeschool for 25 years now. Teamwork is giving and receiving help towards a common goal!

It is important to know that it is very hard to find a mathematically equal contribution by each family member. Life is not pure math or a laboratory with controlled variables. Division of labor and knowing who is supposed to do what efficiently towards a common goal is very important for the smooth functioning of a team. Cohesive communication and learning to be on the same page make the team resonate at the same wavelength to achieve a common goal.

There are times we are disturbed, sad, and angry with things that are happening, and we cannot fix them, for these things we should pray. Praying with pure intentions sends positive energy to a person or predicament. For example, war between countries or racial injustices. Praying makes us feel we are doing well with our thoughts. Prayer is a tremendous coping mechanism and helps us feel connected with Universal energy. When we are not able to help physically, we can listen with kindness and say words with kindness and love. This is like a balm to the person who is going through a rough patch in life.

When people ask me, "How are you so put together?" I tell them that is fake news! I have my autistic days, where I keep myself away from people. I give this example that tickles them. I share that I had heard that when we are upset, we should count to ten before responding. It does not work for me; even counting to a hundred does not work for me. I read somewhere that **"silence is sacred,"** and this worked. Silence helps to create a **space** to disengage and gives us time to cool off. Yogis do "maun brata." The translation to this Sanskrit phrase is "quiet fasting." It means not to use words. This enables the yogi to inculcate self-discipline and mindfulness. **Think of pause as disrupting the domino effect. By just taking away one piece of domino, we stop the cascade.**

We have a rule in the house that each of us has the opportunity to be a unique domino piece, which stops the unrest and anger from perpetuating. When any of us are upset, we say, "I cannot talk right now; give me space." If any of us are so annoyed that we forget the rule, then the person who is the target of that anger says, "We will talk when you are calm!" This strategy works very well because it makes everyone empathetic to each other and receptive to solving the issue. This strategy has worked beautifully because, instead of arguing and getting angry, we are able to talk and resolve issues. We are talking about life, and anyone who tells you that they don't get angry or upset at all, they are either lying, or they are Buddha, the enlightened human being, unicorn among us humans!

I told my yoga guru that I could not stop thinking and worrying despite the daily breathing practices that I was doing. He asked me to sit in a lotus position to focus on the sounds/noises that I hear while breathing normally. In the beginning, I heard all the loud sounds and noises like the noise of traffic and people talking. After a few days of this practice, I started hearing the not-so-loud sounds as well, like dripping water from the faucet, and when I focused more on that sound, then the louder sound/noises seemed to fade away. In this meditative state, I could focus on sounds that are there, but we don't feel them, like my heartbeat and my breathing. Focusing on these rhythmic sounds, "lub-dub" of the heart, and breathing in and out had an extraordinary effect on my mind. I felt as if everything had slowed down, my body felt relaxed, and even though I was awake, I felt the quietness of a sleep-like state. The parrot that was sitting in my head and repeating worrisome stuff was quiet for a while. Once I came out of that yogic moment, I felt recharged and calm. Scientifically, we cannot stop thinking, but with proper breathing and mindfulness, we can slow down the thinking process and give the required respite to the overworking brain.

After self-searching, through introspection, meditation, contemplation, and reflection, we know what causes our anger and what the triggers are, and once we are aware of this, we can develop various means and tools to release anger appropriately. **We may not succeed in proper release of anger every time, but this awareness helps us center back faster. In this process, we also learn to express our genuine apology to others, ability to forgive, and be kind to ourselves.**

Before you start reading the next section of this book, I want you to pause, reflect on what we have read, assimilate the relevant information, and evaluate it for your own energy management needs!

Let's ask ourselves:

---

1. What information mentioned in this section will enhance my energy and happiness?

2. Do I have a need to declutter and simplify my life?

3. Is Physical clutter hindering my energy flow, efficiency, and happiness? What are those? (Make a list).

   • How will I declutter and organize this space for better energy flow and productivity?

4. Is Mental clutter (excessive and redundant thoughts) hindering my energy flow, efficiency, and productivity? What are those?

5. Make a list and address the one thing that you believe is hindering your energy flow and

---

happiness the most. For each physical and mental clutter, apply 3 to 5 interventions that you liked from this book (*I have noticed that too many resolutions results in inertia!*)

SECTION 3:

Healing

"Healing is the return of the memory of wholeness."

- Deepak Chopra

Healing through Kindness

Decluttering helps us create quality in our lives because, by discarding, we learn to work and appreciate what is necessary and important. **Decluttering opens up the space for healing and energy flow!** However, the important question is: **Why do we need to heal?** Without healing, we are broken. Healing makes us whole again-physically, mentally, emotionally, and spiritually. **Healing is the precursor of happiness and health!**

How can we heal? By being kind! First, we must learn to be kind to ourselves because we cannot give what we do not have. How can we be kind to ourselves? We can be kind to ourselves by forgiving ourselves for our mistakes and shortcomings and learning from those mistakes so we can grow into a better person with a loving and kind heart.

How can we be kind to others? Kindness lies in giving. We can give money and time to a cause, and that is an act of kindness. We can give hugs and smiles and check on a friend or a family member. Ask, "How are you doing?" This is an act of kindness. Praying is a universal act of kindness. When we pray for someone, we send positive energy of health, healing, and happiness their way.

How can we learn to be kind? By pausing before reacting. The essence of kindness lies in the pause! For example, when someone is angry, instead of getting upset with them, we should pause and think that maybe they have lost something or someone: a dog, a friend, or a job. *For sure, he has lost his mind for a bit*. This pause gives us that precious moment to respond with kindness. When we think kindly, our words and actions are kind.

Be kind with words! It is important to pause before we load words on our tongue, the softest organ in our body. Words are like missiles because once they are released, they hit the target and break the heart into pieces. On the other hand, words are the most miraculous balm, for they glue every broken piece of the heart. Words of powerful people can bring countries to war or peace. History proves this statement through Hitler and Gandhi. Words matter individually and collectively. Words are the ultimate expression of hate and love!

There is a heart-touching story about how kind words of encouragement helped Albert Einstein to believe in his innate abilities. The story goes like this: when he was in elementary school, his teacher sent a note with him for his mother. His mother burst into tears and said that the teacher had said that Albert is so smart that his teacher is not able to teach him anymore and that Albert was going to change the world. She said she would teach him instead. Later on, after his mother's death, Einstein rediscovered that note. He was a world-renowned physicist by then. The note actually said that Albert was too dumb, and the teacher had refused to teach him. Einstein realized that his mother's kind and loving words of encouragement made him believe in himself, and he did change the world with his theory of relativity!

At this point in time, we need to unite with kindness. After the COVID pandemic, life feels harder. We all are going through collective grief of loss. Loss of life, loss of time, loss of security, and loss of peace of mind. I find that giving hugs and smiles is the easiest way to give kindness. In my talks, I say, "Hugs are the only drugs that we should give away freely!" The audience laughs at this association, and when I also ask them to test it out right there, they all say that they feel good after giving and receiving hugs. What we give comes back to us in many folds!

Kindness for ourselves and to others is the initiation to the healing process. Kindness helps us to love ourselves, and in doing so, we learn to give and receive love! I will talk about love in the chapter "Love is Multifaceted," but before that,

I want to share with you some of my coping skills that have helped me to heal and find happiness!

Healing through Prayer!

We all go through a "why me" phase when we come across trauma or very challenging situations in our lives. We ask God, "Why me?" After Parag's diagnosis, I was lost and lonely, and I, too, asked, "Why me God?" This is a natural reaction to feeling anger, hurt, pain, and/or guilt during this phase of our lives. However, what is not natural, normal, and healthy is to be stuck in this phase forever. My belief in the power of prayer pulled me out of this phase more quickly because I have always believed that prayer helps us heal and gives us courage and hope.

One day, while I was praying, a voice spoke and said, "Parag has autism. Are you going to mope, sulk, and cry, or do something about it?" In that moment I felt enormous courage. I did not know what I was going to do, but I knew that I was not going to mope, sulk, and cry! Later, I realized that the Divine voice was asking me to change my worries to concern! Worries are making the mountain out of molehill; in our minds, we see dreary things, but we do nothing about it. **Worry is the biggest dissipator of energy**. Concerns are taking the first step forward, changing something about the challenging situation that we are facing and doing something about it.

When Parag was little, I used to worry about a lot of things, and one of the things that I used to worry about was *how I will teach him to shave*. I used to think that he would give me a very hard time making him shave, and then I would project my mind to the future. In my mind's eye, I would see Parag rolling on the floor, crying, throwing tantrums, cutting his face, and bleeding all over. These thoughts were very worrisome and dissipated my energy. It made me irritable and unhappy because the future seemed bleak, miserable, and gloomy.

In my talks, I share Parag's first video of shaving, and everyone laughs because he is happily shaving away and admiring himself in the mirror. I guess he had observed his dad and Ankur shave. He was ready to learn with gusto. While Parag was shaving happily, I wished I had not worried so much when he was little. You can watch this video on the Facebook Page, "Autism Our Journey and Finding Happiness." I shared it with the article I have written, **"Change Worries to Concerns."**

By worrying, all I did was make my present moment miserable and unhappy, for the future did not unfold as I had imagined. This makes me share a wisdom that comes from the movie King Fu Panda: "Yesterday is a history, tomorrow is a mystery, today is a gift, that is why it is called present!" It is a powerful message because it is asking us to be right here, right now. By doing so, we stop worrying about what has happened in the past and what is going to happen in the future, and we are right here in the present, doing something about the predicament we are facing. Once we stay in the present, we start learning to change worries into concerns! Leo Buscaglia has beautifully said,

"Worry never robs tomorrow of its sorrow; it only saps today of its joy."

My grandma always said that when things don't go our way, it is going God's way. God has a better plan that we cannot see all the time. She told me this story, and when things are not going as I plan, it gives me solace and patience. The story goes like this: There was a king, and his best friend was also his adviser. He was wise, and he said, "Things happen for good." One day, the king and his friend went on a hunting trip, and there was an accident. The king lost his little finger. The king was very upset and asked his friend what was good about losing his finger. This hasn't happened for good. The king's advisor friend said that it has happened for good, but we can't see that right now. The king was very upset and ordered his soldiers to put his advisor friend into a dungeon. After a few months, the king went for a hunting trip alone, and savages kidnapped the king to sacrifice him. When they saw that the king did not have a little finger, they let him go because they could not sacrifice anyone who had physical imperfection. When the king came back to his kingdom, he released his advisor friend from the dungeon. The king said, "You were right; if I had not lost my little finger, the savages would have sacrificed me." The king said that he could see how losing his little finger turned out to be a good thing for him, but definitely not a good thing for his advisor friend because he was put away in the dungeon. The advisor friend said, "Thank God! If I was with you on this hunting trip, the savages would have sacrificed me!"

This is a simple story, yet it powerfully conveys the message that incidences we perceive as negative and detrimental may not be so; something good is hidden that we don't see at that time.

When I was little, I asked my great aunt, "Why does God not answer my prayers?". She said that He is always answering our prayers, but we don't see or listen carefully.

When we pray with pure heart, God answers our prayers, but many times, we do not see the help He sends our way. Let me tell you a story to clarify this. There was a flood, and a man was stranded on a rooftop. He fervently prayed for God to help him. Some people came to him on a boat and asked him to hop on that boat, but this man refused and went on praying. Then, after a while, a helicopter came by and let down the ladder so he could climb up, but the man kept on praying. He went on praying and drowned in the flood. When he went to heaven, he asked God, "Why did you not come to save me?" God smiled and said, "I sent you help twice, but you refused to take it." The gist of the story is that God answers our prayers, and seeing the answers to our prayers is important. In the chapter, "Advice from the Pediatrician" in my book, *Autism Our Journey and Finding Happiness*, I have written "...I was at the brink of emotional and physical breakdown. I called Parag's pediatrician, and, to this day, I believe that God spoke to me through him" (*Autism Our Journey and Finding Happiness*, chapter: Advice from the Pediatrician, page 21). His advice to make our household "as normal as possible" became a guiding force for me in dealing with Parag's autism.

My prayers have evolved with time.

> "I am spiritual and believe in the power of prayers. The beauty of praying is that it can happen anytime and anywhere. As I pray more and more, my prayer has evolved too. My father, a philosopher and an avid believer in the power of prayer, had told me that praying channels our positive energy, and

through the power of prayer, we heal, find inner peace, and contentment. Initially, I asked God to do things for me or, better put, fix things for me. I would also pray for others and ask Him to fix things for them. Then, one fine day, it dawned on me that God helps those who help themselves. So, I started actively doing something about whatever I wanted to be different. This also made me thankful for all the blessings that God has bestowed on me. Once I was able to count my blessings, I was able to deal with things with a positive frame of mind and tremendous gusto. "(*Autism Our Journey and Finding Happiness, Chapter 3- Parag's Diagnosis and My Cleansing*)

Praying is not mechanical chanting of God's name, holy books, or quoting verses. Kabir, a Sufi saint, has written this couplet: "Mala Pherat Jug Bhaya, Phira Na Man Ka Pher, Kar Ka Manaka Daar De, Man Ka Manaka Pher." The translation is, "We go on praying on the rosary mechanically for ages, without changing our corrupted thinking. We should leave the rosary and change our thinking!" The quality of thoughts matters in connecting meaningfully with God.

During difficult times, praying and understanding that nothing is permanent helps. Knowing that "this too shall pass" gives us hope and fortitude to deal with hardships. When things are going well, praying and thanking God helps us appreciate the blessings that he has bestowed on us even more. **Prayer is the common denominator between all religions. It is a unifying factor for humanity!**

Gardening Healed Me

"Gardening not only turned me from a city girl to an avid farmer but gave me a new eye to appreciate nature, and I just marvel at being a part of the immense drama. My yogic moments have come by being one with nature. It gives me the absolute peace and, therefore, the energy and the enthusiasm to deal, not just with autism, but life itself." (*Autism Our Journey and Finding Happiness;* chapter Parag's diagnosis and my cleansing; page 19)

Connecting Mother Earth through gardening has helped me channel my thoughts and is instrumental in my healing. In times of distress, every kid seeks their mother; I unknowingly turned to Mother Earth for solace. When Parag was diagnosed, I was desolate, nothing was making sense, and one day, in a moment of sheer hopelessness, while sitting in my backyard on the grass, I found a stick, and I started digging. I was crying in desperation and pleading for help from the Universe. Little did I know that my prayers were reaching the Universal All-pervasive energy. It was listening to my plea for help, and it organically prodded me to dig a piece of land.

As I dug the ground, I felt that my pain was releasing to the ground, and I continued to dig. When I was done, I had blisters in my palm, but I felt better. "The physical labor seemed to soothe the mental chaos that I was facing" (*Autism Our Journey and Finding Happiness*, chapter Parag's diagnosis and my cleansing, page 18). The repetitive movement of digging gave me peace and calm. I decided to buy a spade, shovel, and trowel to dig more! In this moment, I, a city girl, turned into a farmer! I dug a small patch of ground, and then, by default, I decided to plant vegetables. I had never done gardening; this was a unique experience that took birth organically.

Gardening not only helped with my emotional cleansing by revealing the bigger picture of our interconnectivity on this Earth, but it has also helped me understand many of the behavioral conditions of Autism and how to approach it. Repetitive actions calm us down when we are stressed. That is why when we pray or chant mantras repetitively, it helps us to refocus, it is calming, and it grounds us to the task at hand. Thus, experiencing the calming effect on my distraught nerves through the repetitive action of praying and gardening helped me realize that Parag and many kids with autism stem and display repetitive behavior to calm themselves down. The world around them is disorderly and constantly changing, and the repetitive movement of stemming helps them. **It is ironic that the answer to one of my questions as to why Parag stems came from my own actively pursuing a repetitive action of digging for solace.**

Knowing that stemming is an inbuilt coping mechanism, I did not stop Parag from displaying those repetitive behaviors, but I let him express those through more socially acceptable behaviors. For example, when Parag was little, he used to flap his hand, and it drew negative public attention. I taught him to put his hands in his trouser pockets. He was still trying to flap his hands inside the pockets, but now it did not draw negative public attention. Gradually, he stopped flapping his hands. **Why did his hand flapping, repetitive behavior, or stemming become extinguished**? The answer that came to me was that when Parag put his hands in the pockets, the brain was still sending the signals to his hands, but now the brain was not getting the gratification in the degree as before because it is harder to flap hands freely in the pockets. So, over time, the signal to the hands became weaker, both in intensity and in frequency. Eventually, the brain stopped sending the signal to the hands, and this behavior was extinguished. I have extinguished another symptomatic behavior, Parag's toe walking. Many kids with autism walk on their toes. Many neurotypical toddlers do that too, but they get out of it on their own, while many toddlers with autism never do. I got hard-soled shoes for Parag, and the signal of the brain to the toes got weaker and weaker until it was extinguished. **I believe this is a huge behavioral discovery in the field of** autism that restricted expression of the behaviors subdues it and even extinguishes it over time.

Gardening taught me to have hope. When we sow the seeds for a long time, we feel that nothing is happening, but that is not true. We must go on watering that piece of land and make sure that it is receiving sunlight. Then, the miracle that was happening under the Earth reveals itself, and we see the birth of saplings, the birth of new life. Gardening taught me that once I put in work, I should wait patiently even though many times the result of the work was not discernible immediately. **Hope is the driving force behind working patiently and with perseverance.**

Weeding the garden is important because weeds take the same nutrients and space that the seeds need to grow. Weeds grow extremely fast, stifling the growth of seeds. Similarly, we need to weed off negative thoughts because they are **parasitic** in nature. They invade our physical and mental space, and in doing so, they stunt our physical, mental, emotional, and spiritual growth. "Once I took away the weeds of anger and bitterness, my heart started growing with understanding, love, and compassion. This wisdom gave me the ability to compartmentalize my life, allocate time to everyone and to myself and be happy and to see the beautiful and ignore the ugly. It was an absolute turn for me. (*Autism Our Journey and Finding Happiness*, Chapter Parag's diagnosis and my cleansing, page 17)

Gardening taught me an important lesson of how to share so that we can benefit each other. Sharing has to be symbiotic because it helps the plants share the same space, which is beneficial to each other and to the entire community! When we went to Machu Picchu in Peru, the train ride from Cusco into the Sacred Valley through the Amazon Forest was spectacular. What struck me was thousands and thousands of breath-taking orchids growing on the limbs of the trees. Orchids are epiphytes, and they live symbiotically on a tree. Both the tree and the orchid benefit from this coexistence. The strong tree helps the orchid with sturdy support for the orchid to grow on the branches and the trunk of the tree. This allows it to get sunlight for photosynthesis. Being high up also protects them from being eaten by the ground-dwelling animals. Orchids, like other epiphytes, absorb excess water or moisture from the air and do not let the roots of the tree have too much water, which can lead to root rotting. It also regulates temperature fluctuation by maintaining the vapor pressure, and when the epiphytes die, they decompose and become fertilizer to the soil around the tree. This allows it to remain healthy and strong. All through its life, the orchid makes the tree look extraordinarily beautiful. I may not have admired those gigantic trees as much without those eye-catching orchids on them.

The epiphytes help not only the ecophysiology of the tree but also the ecosystem of the forest itself. The presence of epiphytes indicates that the ecosystem of the forest and the entire community is vibrant, healthy, and lively. **Symbiosis is a beautiful lesson from Mother Nature about giving, taking, sharing, and enhancing each other to bring overall balance and harmony in our lives.** I may not have imbibed this lesson if I was not an avid gardener and connected to Mother Earth.

Harvesting is the most joyous moment for a farmer because he reaps the fruit of his labor. The joy of harvesting my organic vegetables made me share the produce with my friends and family, and it also gave birth to a new hobby: cooking. Both my sons and my husband are foodies, and cooking for them became even more pleasurable and creative with the produce from my garden. Gradually, the process of cooking, too, has become therapy for me.

Harvesting has a much deeper meaning in our lives. My grandma used to say, "Jaisi karni waisi bharni." This is the Hindi version of English saying, "you reap what you sow". When I asked her the meaning, she gave a concrete example and said, "If you grow bitter melon and expect it to taste like mangoes, it is stupidity." I agreed with this irrefutable example and wondered who could be so stupid. Later in life, I realized that I didn't know about others, but I definitely knew myself. In my mind's garden, I was sowing weeds of negativity, which is what I was reaping, but I wanted to reap positive results. When we sow the seed of love, we reap love and spread it too. **Gardening gave me the wisdom to understand that we are all connected and that we are all seeds on Mother Earth. Our natural purpose, just like any seed, is to grow, propagate, give, and then be one with Universal All-pervasive Energy.**

Healing with a Sense of Humor

I have not met a person yet who doesn't want to be happy. Developing a sense of humor helps us to be happy. Funny things are happening throughout the day, but we fail to see them as funny because we are uptight in our own thoughts about the future or about the past. This takes away our ability to have fun and laugh at little things that are happening in the present. To inculcate a sense of humor, all we have to do is loosen up and see the lighter side of things.

When we inculcate a sense of humor, the journey of life becomes fun and pleasurable in spite of the challenges. When we see the funny side of things or think of memories that make us smile or laugh, it works like a cooling balm for everyone, particularly for caregivers who are taking care of loved ones day in and day out with no break.

In dealing with Parag's autism, I had to learn to smile and sometimes laugh at circumstances that were ludicrous! Life is short, but for us who are dealing with extraordinary challenges, our days are long! One antidote to deal with serious challenges is to develop a sense of humor. You must be familiar with the song in the classic movie Mary Poppins, "Spoon full of sugar helps the medicine go down." A sense of humor is nothing but a symbolic spoon full of sugar, which helps the challenges to go down!

About four years back, Parag started throwing the entire gallon of milk into the sink. I realized that he was stimming (creating stimulation); he liked seeing milk go down the drain in a circular motion! The intervention was to make him pour the milk into the glass, drink it, and then keep the milk jar in the fridge. Once he did that, I praised him exuberantly for the good job of keeping back the milk. I started keeping enough milk for him to pour in the glass and just a little bit more to keep back in the fridge. If he threw the milk, it would not be a big waste, and with a small amount of milk spilled in the sink, he could not stim because a little bit of milk goes down the drain very fast without making the circular motion.

Any behavioral intervention demands a lot of patience and perseverance from the caregivers. Since I thought of it as a game, it did not rile me. The day Parag threw the milk, I thought of it as he won and accepted his win with a smile. The day he did not, I celebrated my win with a grin.

This is just one example of many. I tell everyone, thanks to Parag, that excitement is maintained in my house, and there is never a boring moment. In the Facebook page, *Autism Our Journey and Finding Happiness,*" I have shared Parag's video of stealing Raisins under the title "Parag got caught red-handed with mouthful of raisins." It was funny to me because when I said stealing is a bad thing and that he should not steal. After all that teaching and preaching, when I asked him if he would do this again, he smiled and said, "Yes!" I couldn't stop laughing at his honesty. In my house, the Tom and Jerry situation often happens between Parag and me. "Laughter is the best medicine," and Parag makes us laugh with his innocent pranks.

Can we develop a sense of humor? I believe we can once we start seeing the funny side of things. I was amazed to witness "Laughter yoga" practice. When I was visiting my parents in India, I saw some people gathering in a park, and they all started making a laughing sound, "ha-ha," in a continuous chorus. Soon, all of them were not fake laughing but actually laughing. I, along with other joggers who had stopped to watch, was smiling while watching them laugh. That day, I realized laughter is infectious, for it captures a happy state of mind, and we all desire that state of mind. That day, I literally witnessed "fake it till you make it".

Challenges can knock us down, but a sense of humor makes us bounce back! When we fall and we can laugh at it, it loses its sting. Developing the ability to laugh at things that go differently than we had planned makes us resilient and happy. **Laughing at ourselves and finding things to laugh about is the art of being happy!**

Healing from
Criticism and Senseless Competition

When someone criticizes us, we feel we are put under a microscope to be dissected. I remember dissecting a frog in high school; it was pinned and dead, so the poor creature did not feel the pain of dissection. However, criticism is a dissection of a person who is very much alive and under the lens, that is, human eyes. No one likes to be criticized because we feel that the person who is criticizing us is finding faults in us. Criticism comes from a place of control and superiority.

Why does criticism hurt us? **We want everyone to like us.** This is an undue expectation. Let me share a story that I heard when I was a kid. There was a man and his son going to the market to sell their donkey. People saw them and said what is the point of a donkey if one doesn't ride on it. So, the man sat his son on the donkey, and, as they went along, some people saw them and chided at the boy. They said that he should be ashamed of himself, that he is able-bodied and sitting on the donkey while his old dad is walking on his foot. Now, both the dad and son sat on the donkey. After a while, some people saw them and commented that they were so cruel to the donkey and that they should be ashamed of overburdening the poor animal. The man and his son felt that they had to rectify their mistake of being unjust to the donkey, so they tied the donkey upside down by the pole and carried it. People who saw them were making fun of them, and the donkey was horrified and started kicking. They were on the bridge, the rope of the donkey's hind-leg came off, and it slipped off the pole into the river. Since its front feet were still tied, it drowned and died. It is a sad story. **The moral of the story is that when we try to please everyone so that they will like us, we end up being unhappy.**

A few years back, a friend told me that she wanted to share with me what a common friend had told her about me. I said that I did not need to know. If it was good, she just heard nice things about me, and if it was not good, then she got entertained. I know true friends always have our backs! Knowing who we are and having **self-esteem** helps us defeat negative criticisms and gossip.

Not all criticism is negative. Our well-wishers want us to be happy; their criticism comes from their pure intention to help us. Well-wishers don't find faults in us; they direct us to overcome our shortcomings and build us into stronger people. This is a positive criticism or constructive criticism! Positive criticism is feedback, an input to help us become better. People who give positive criticism do not criticize the person, but they criticize the situation. Many grandparents come to my talks and conferences because they are taking care of their grandchildren with autism. I am amazed at their resilience in understanding and helping their grandchildren. They love their grandkids, and they criticize the situation due to autism, but they never criticize their grandkids. These grandmothers are absolutely "grand," for they teach me the true meaning of caring!

How can we not be affected by negative criticism? When we accept that we have faults, we are not perfect. Remembering that the person who criticizes us is not perfect either helps because this thought is a leveling ground. People who criticize us negatively find faults in us because of their bloated egos and definitely are not kind. We let them be the judge of our character. Once we know that, we don't become a good person or a bad person because someone says so. One of the biggest things about being affected by negative criticism is that we give too much importance to what others are thinking about us. **What we think and knowing who we are makes us comfortable in our own skin, and this empowers us to deflect negative criticism.**

Is competition a negative or positive endeavor? Competition itself is neither good nor bad. The intention

behind it, or the mindset behind the competition, makes it positive or negative. If competition evokes jealousy and rivalry, it is bad because these are negative emotions. When we compete with ourselves, it is the most beautiful thing that happens to us. This means we are in sync with our innate talent. Developing talent is our calling. Albert Einstein said, "Everyone is a genius, but if you judge a fish by its ability to climb a tree. It would live its life believing it is stupid." This means that we all can be geniuses, provided we find our habitat for our innate talent

The problem is that in this society, a kid is exposed to competing with others rather than getting to know their own abilities. My elder son Ankur was in the swim team for the Gadsden Swimming Cub, and one day I said to him, "Don't you feel bad that a girl beat you to hold the first place?" He looked me in the eye and said, "No, she is better than me!" In that moment I felt ashamed that I was instilling a gender bias in him and at the same time felt so proud of him that he was above that. A nine-year-old kid taught me a huge lesson about true competition. When I was growing up in India, gender bias was rampant. India is largely a patriarchal society, so gender bias is ingrained culturally, and I, too, had picked this by sheer osmosis of growing up there.

How can we learn to compete without rivalry and jealousy?

The role of a guide and a teacher is very important in inculcating our innate talent and in coming out of our shells. When I was in third grade, my classroom teacher, Mrs. John, asked us to name our friends. When my turn came, I told her that "I had no friends." She immediately contradicted me and said that she was my friend and that I should eat lunch with her in the classroom. She and her two kids ate lunch in the classroom. During the lunch break, while we all ate lunch, she taught us songs and told us stories I still remember. Once I graduated from her class, I started making friends on my own and also became a voracious reader. I was no longer a shy child; she had taught me one of the biggest lessons of my life: **to explore and reach out**! A teacher, a guru, and a guide are role models, and they can change a kid's life and make them learn to compete with themselves and bring out their innate talent!

We should strive to find role models. When we think of the people who inspire us because of certain attributes and qualities, we don't want to beat them, but we are motivated to learn from them and improve ourselves. This allows us to compete with ourselves and enhance the abilities we want to improve, and this inculcates growth and happiness.

My grandma used to say that when we look at other people's plates of food, we forget to appreciate what God has put in ours. There is a huge lesson in this. When we compete blindly, we forget to enjoy our own gifts and blessings. Learning to see and find our innate gifts and qualities helps us not compete with others but with ourselves and go on the path of self-improvement and self-enhancement. This makes us happy and content!

Healing and Growing from Failure!

Failure is when we do not reach the desired outcome! It is subjective, and failure hurts our self-worth. Sometimes, failing hurts badly, so much so that we think it is too late and nothing can be done. This is not true because life is made of multiple chances. Alexander Graham Bell said, "When one door closes, another one opens," but we often look so long and regretfully upon the closed door that we do not see the ones that are open for us.

I believe failure is when we stop trying to improve upon the mistakes that we make. This means we give up, and that is a failure indeed. When we don't accept failure, then we work harder and smarter to reach the desired goal, and it also allows us to explore other opportunities that we do not think about until we fail. "To err is human", but when we learn from it, we grow into a better human being, a better version of ourselves. Henry Ford said, "Failure is simply the opportunity to begin again, this time more intelligently."

We fail and we break because we are rigid. When Parag was diagnosed, I told my dad that everything seemed to be falling apart and that the entire future seemed bleak. He told me to adapt, and I asked him how. My dad said, "Be like bamboo!" I just stared at him because the meaning eluded me. He smiled and said, "When there is a storm, bamboo sways with the storm and, due to its flexibility, it does not break. The same storm breaks huge trees because they are stiff." He said, "flexibility brings resilience." I understood the nuance of adaptation that day; according to the situation, we have to learn to mold ourselves to survive the challenges and crises that life throws our way. To succeed, we have to be flexible, wanting to change, mold, adapt, and that makes us resilient. Resilience imparts tenacity and determination to push through and not accept failure.

Failure and success are determined by whether we are dreaming or daydreaming! There is a huge difference between having a dream and daydreaming. Usain Bolt has concisely stated, "Dreams are free. Goals have a cost. While you can daydream for free, goals don't come without a price. Time, effort, sacrifice, and sweat. How will you pay for your goals?" Daydreaming is a recipe for failure because we go on thinking and making all the grand plans in our heads without acting upon them. My grandma told a story about a daydreamer. There was a very pretty girl in a village. She had some hens that gave eggs, and she sold the eggs for her livelihood. She wanted to become rich and always daydreamed about various ways to become rich. One day, she took the eggs to the market, holding the basket full of eggs on her head. She started daydreaming that she was going to the market, and a rich merchant saw her and fell in love with her for her beauty. He asked her to marry him, but she was not going to marry him because he was not rich enough, and she was going to marry the king, the richest person in that kingdom. So, she shook her head to reject the merchant's proposal for marriage. The basket full of eggs slipped from her head when she shook her head, and that made her come out of her daydream to see that all her eggs were broken, and so was her goal to become rich. Daydreams or procrastination take away our energy to move forward with focused action.

Having a dream is diametrically opposite to daydreaming. Eleanor Roosevelt said, "The future belongs to those who believe in the beauty of their dreams." It is a very powerful thing to have because people who have dreamed and acted upon their dreams have changed the course of history. Martin Luther King is a shining example; his words "I have a dream" continue to give courage to fight injustice and biases in society.

We fail because we have partial knowledge but think we know all. The story of the six blind men who wanted to know what the elephant looked like explains the mindset. The first one touched the leg and said the elephant is like a pillar. The second one touched the tail and said the elephant is like a rope. The third blind man touched the ear and said that the elephant is like a fan. The fourth one touched the trunk and said it was like a branch of a tree. The fifth one touched the belly and said the elephant is like a wall, and the sixth one touched the tusk and said it is like a spear. They were arguing among themselves, so they sought the help of a person who could see how to sort out their confusion and the argument. The sighted person listened to them and then said that they all were correct, but they all touched different parts of the elephant, and their view is limited to what they experienced. This story is symbolic; half knowledge is a dangerous thing because it makes our mind blind, and we do not see things with clarity. We fail because we don't expand our horizons! Limited knowledge is like knowing the road map partially, which will take us so far but never to the desired destination.

Success is no coincidence; it is consistent and persistent hard work. Chugging along with dogged determination. Luck is disciplined hard work! When people call someone lucky, they just see success, the outward manifestation of hard work. They don't see the toil and sacrifices that have gone into making that person successful. Someone asked me, "If hard work brings luck, then a rickshaw driver works hard, toils long hours, and corporate employee who works same hours, makes good money, and has a lavish lifestyle. How do you explain that? I said, "The drive to change the situation sets people apart and that money is not equal to success." Ishwar Chandra Vidyasagar was born in abject poverty; he used to study under the streetlamp because his parents could not afford an oil lamp. His drive for knowledge not only pulled him out of abject poverty, but he also made social changes in 19th century Indian society. He was the visionary who made widow remarriage possible in India, which was forbidden at that time. He became a huge advocate for education for all. He was given the honorific title of "Vidyasagar," which means "ocean of knowledge."

I believe it was not luck but dogged determination to tweak every setback that made Thomas Alva Edison invent a lightbulb! After nine hundred and ninety-nine attempts, Thomas Edison succeeded in perfecting the light bulb. He went on improving without giving up or giving in, and we all are reaping the benefit of his fortitude and invention, the light bulb. In the words of Edison, "genius is one percent inspiration and ninety-nine percent perspiration." When a journalist asked him how it feels to have failed 1000 times in inventing the incandescent light bulb? Edison said, "I didn't fail 1,000 times. The light bulb was an invention with 1,000 steps." It is said that Edison was working on this project for 15 hours every day, 5 hours problem solving and 10 hours executing it until he succeeded. His story inspires me, and I hope it inspires you too.

Failure and success lie in our attitude. The pessimist finds reasons outside themselves for their failure- bad luck, destiny, unsupportive people, and uncongenial situations! The optimist looks inside themselves for their failures and analyzes what made them not avail the opportunity. They ask what changes they need to foster to get the desired results. How can I get there? After reflecting, they gradually build themselves with renewed perspective and positivity to make their dream a reality. Success is a cumulative effect of tweaking every failure until it is not a failure. We stop the loop of failures the day we decide to own our failures; we acknowledge our mistakes and take responsibility for them. This acknowledgment makes us fix our weaknesses, build ourselves, and work harder and smarter to get the desired results.

Sometimes, no matter how much work we put in, we don't succeed, and the reason could be that we are not improving upon the mistakes we have made in the past. Einstein has said, "Insanity is doing the same thing over and over and expecting different results." So, the crux lies in learning from our mistakes and improving upon them. We know the idiom, "practice makes perfect". I disagree; I believe perfect practice makes perfect. It is not neuroscience to understand that wrong practice, no matter how much we practice, will not give us success. When we practice correctly, the outcome is favorable.

We caregivers do the same tasks again and again in taking care of our loved ones, and sometimes it makes us impatient and hopeless. This story helps me quell my impatience and reenergizes me with the thought that there is a bigger purpose for every small thing we do. Only by doing the work diligently and with patience will the bigger picture one day be revealed. The story goes like this: There was a monastery, and the priests were making a huge tapestry. Everyone had to weave a different color yarn in a certain pattern. One priest went to the head priest and said I am tired of weaving yellow thread the whole day; it is so boring; it seems meaningless and redundant. The head priest asked him to go on doing his task and said that the meaning would reveal itself. When the priests finished their work, all the pieces of the tapestry were sewn together and the priest who had found his work meaningless, boring, and repetitive fell on his knees and started crying, for when all the pieces of the tapestry was sewn together, he realized that he was weaving the halo around Christ's head. In that moment, it dawned upon him that he was part of a masterful creation, and his yellow yarn was the crowning glory adorning Christ's head. We may not see the bigger picture right away, but by going on and doing our part, it reveals to us that our action is a part of a bigger picture. We give up too soon to let it reveal to us!

Most of the time, things don't go the way I plan. In raising Parag, I have felt, and sometimes still feel, the dark thoughts of failure engulfing me. Progress with Parag is so slow that many days, I feel like I am stuck. I feel I am stuck in a predicament like Sisyphus, rolling the boulder that always slides down the mountain, never succeeding, always struggling. This thought generates sadness and anger toward the injustice of this situation of incurable disorder, Autism. On days like these, I have to look back, and that takes away the doubt that I am stuck. I have been running Parag's homeschool for twenty-five years now. Consistent and persistent efforts have paid off. Progress is slow, but we are not stuck for sure! I also look for inspiration to shake me out of these somber thoughts. I make myself think of parents, who are heroes in my eyes, who have a special needs kid who cannot move; they feed them with tubes and change diapers. I look up to them with no respect but reverence. Seeing their dedication and chugging along in spite of their herculean challenge centers me and inspires me to get my act together. Once I shifted my focus from what I don't have to what I have, inculcating a thankful heart and counting my blessings slowly but surely started healing me, building me, and giving me energy and enthusiasm for the journey ahead.

I have written:

> "Two things that I watched on television gave me immense courage and willpower in putting a brave front against autism. I saw a man with one leg climb Mount Everest. I understood that our mind has to believe, and then our body can be trained to follow the mission. The second thing that I saw on the television was that the scientists had trained a parrot to do various tricks by making it do the task repeatedly. I thought a parrot's brain is so tiny compared to human brain, if the neural wiring in the brain is not working properly as in autism, it can be made to work way beyond imagination by repeated training," (*Autism Our Journey and Finding Happiness,* chapter Parag's diagnosis and my cleansing page 17).

One of the approaches to teaching reading to students is called **DEAR- Drop Everything and Read**. In the classroom setting, the teacher asks the students to stop whatever they are doing and pick up a book of their liking from the bookshelf and read for a while. We should apply this in life, not just for reading, but to prioritize something that is important and needs to be done. We need to drop whatever we are involved in and pick up what needs to be done- Drop Everything and Act! Prioritizing helps us feel content and happy. When trying to juggle all the tasks, the probability of failing is higher than succeeding, and even when we succeed, chances are we never get to enjoy the process because we are like headless chickens while performing the work!

My CrossFit Coach said that there are two kinds of students. There are those to whom you say, "You can't do it," and they will prove the teacher wrong. The other kind is if you tell them, "You can't do it," they will believe it and stop doing the work. He said, "Mamta, it is important for a coach to know which kind of student one is training and motivate them accordingly."

I am a mother of a special needs kid who believes in giving care with positive encouragement! My gardening instinct deciphered his words differently; every plant is unique, and they need a different degree of water, sunlight, and fertilizer to grow. If we water the cactus too much, it will die; it needs arid land with a lot of sunlight to grow. If we plant a mango tree, a tropical plant, in a desert, it will not grow. Thus, unlocking the potential energy, that is, the innate ability, requires the right environment with the right nurturing. Every parent is a gardener of their children, but to become a caregiver, we have to know how to nurture their innate talent and unlock the potential energy!

How do we know that we have grown from failures? Physical growth is discernible. We are born, we grow into adults, and then we grow old. However, our mental, emotional, and spiritual growth is not visible outwardly all the time. Growth lies in acknowledging failure and then constantly improving and adapting towards the desired goal. I often tell my son, Ankur, "Lage raho Munna Bhai," (translation- "keep going Munna Bhai."). This makes him smile and encourages him. This is a line from a Hindi comedy movie with a message of kindness and being strong in spite of adversities. Growth is guiding without being didactic. When we can redirect someone to something funny yet inspiring, it helps them to not only relieve the stress of failure and setbacks but also encourages them to be strong.

When we are feeling low due to setbacks and failures, calming our mind is essential to regrouping and recharging. Everyone has their own coping mechanism to handle these moments. I like to watch feel-good and inspiring movies. I recently saw a movie, "Cool Runnings," which is a humorous portrayal of four Jamaican youth determined to participate in the bobsleigh competition in the 1998 Winter Olympics. Everyone laughed at them, but that did not deter them, and they participated as well. Even though they did not win any Olympic medals, they proved their mettle and were celebrated as heroes not just in Jamaica but by the entire world. This movie is inspiring, and it brings forth a message that not winning doesn't mean failing, but the honest hard work to play the best game, in spite of all the odds, is what counts.

Growth is understanding that failures are not roadblocks but multiple opportunities to improve and learn. **The Litmus paper test of growth is when given the same or similar circumstances, we respond rather differently with less anxiety and with a better attitude.** Last April, in 2023, a month before my Annual Autism Conference, "Together We Can Make a Difference," Parag's teacher quit the homeschool due to a challenging situation at her home. I felt overwhelmed by the pressure of organizing the conference and running Parag's homeschool without any help. This year in 2024, history repeated itself, and the teacher I had trained to help me run Parag's homeschool left suddenly in March due to a challenging pregnancy. I prayed for guidance and grace and did not feel as disturbed. I went on running Parag's school, and, with God's grace, we found a young, enthusiastic, and kind lady; while training her to be Parag's teacher, I could plan the conference, and thankfully, I was not as anxious. I was able to handle the same situation better because, this time, I could compartmentalize myself. Compartmentalization is a huge sign of growth. This means we know how to be present at the moment with the task at hand. To be in the moment is hard practice but worth practicing because it balances us and keeps us grounded.

Resilience in times of hardship is a sign of growth. The saying that a smooth sea never made a skilled sailor is true. We don't have to go looking for challenges, but when it comes our way, instead of blaming it on destiny or others, if we take charge of it, we evolve and grow as a person. Facing challenges sharpens our problem-solving and critical thinking skills. It also makes us appreciate what we have, and we learn to count our blessings. It makes us humble and kind!

Asking for help from the right person at the right time is a sign of emotional growth. I am a multitasking mama with two hands, trying to be Durga, the goddess with eight hands. Now, I know that my "tribe" is my hands. Their presence and support make the journey of life into an adventure. Growth is knowing that life tests our endurance, like a marathon. We cannot run a marathon with the mindset of a sprint runner. In training for a marathon, my husband and I learned to conserve energy, replenish the depleted electrolytes, and prevent energy depletion. In the same way, in life, we have to reenergize through positive thinking and learn to pace ourselves! Growth lies in learning to pause and enjoy every milestone with our loved ones, our friends, and our family. This makes us happy and reenergizes us for the journey ahead!

I have shared in the chapter Shedding Confusion and Finding Direction that when I asked for advice from my dad after Parag's diagnosis, "How am I going to live my life? My life ahead feels so gloomy. I am so confused." He smiled and said, **"No confusion, no learning."** Twenty-five years later, I am humbly adding to his advice, **"No failure, no learning!"**

Healing and Taking Care of the Body

For our overall well-being, to feel good, energetic, and happy, a healthy body is a must. A healthy body contributes to increasing the quality of our lives. The body is a marvelous complex biological machine. We breathe, we blink, our heart beats, and we are not even aware of these functions until we are sick. For example, we never think about how we breathe until we are down with a mere common cold. When we are physically not well, even with minor stuff like cough and cold, aches and pains, we don't feel like doing anything because we don't feel good. Our energy plummets, and we are not able to enjoy life. Therefore, taking care of the body is a must because a healthy mind resides in a healthy body!

Sleeping helps the body heal! Sleeping is Nature's blessing to all living things. Sleeping is essential for the rejuvenation of the body and mind. Every living thing has an inbuilt circadian rhythm, a biological clock that runs twenty-four hours and regulates sleep and wakefulness. Sleep and rest are important for the conservation of energy. Just like a computer needs rebooting, so do our body and brain. After a good night's sleep, we feel refreshed and rejuvenated because we heal in our sleep. Sleep helps fix the wear and tear of our hardware, the brain, and the body. Sleep allows the software, our mind, to reorganize information and memories so that when we wake up, we can work or act with clarity and purpose. The idiom *early to bed and early to rise makes a man healthy, wealthy, and wise, and it* is a pearl of wisdom indeed. My husband and I follow this idiom, and I have found out that waking up early gives us an early start for the day and so much more time to accomplish the work for the day without hurry, and productivity increases as well.

Taking care of our bodies by **grooming and hygiene** helps us prevent infections, improve our immune system, and develop discipline, self-esteem, and confidence. We are the only animal that cuts nails and hair and wears clothes. This level of grooming separates humans from the other species of the animal kingdom. Being clean, groomed, presentable, and looking our best helps to boost our self-image and confidence.

We take care of our bodies by eating healthy and heartily! We live in a culture of gluttony. Eating has become a habit. We eat whether we are hungry or not. Out of habit, we eat breakfast, lunch, dinner, munch, and drink all kinds of unnecessary sugary liquids.

Coming from a Brahmin background from Mithila, my ancestors lived a lifestyle of "simple living and high thinking." Fasting was built into their lifestyle. My grandma ate once a day, around four in the afternoon. I asked her why she eats once a day. She said that she eats at this time because that is when she is done with her daily chores; she is relaxed and hungry. Therefore, eating in the late afternoon, she enjoys the food thoroughly. When we are hungry, food tastes great, and we are satisfied and nourished. She told me a story that I am sharing with you. Many students who learned from a renowned guru lived in an ashram. One day, when the student asked the guru to eat, he said, "Kheer (rice pudding) is cooking; I will eat when it is fully cooked." The students got excited that there was this treat that was being cooked in the ashram kitchen. The guru sat down to eat and ate what the students had eaten: rice, daal, and vegetables. They asked the guru when he would eat kheer, for they all thought that once the guru eats this delicious dessert, they will get to have it too. The guru said, "I already ate kheer." The students said that he had just eaten the food they all had. Guru said, "Yes, but I waited until I was so hungry that it gave me the same satisfaction that kheer would have given me."

The yogis had found out that fasting and eating just enough to give fuel to the body lead to a healthy life with longevity. There is an ancient saying in Sanskrit, "ekam bhuktam yogi," or *yogi eats once a day*. "Dwi bhuktam bhogi," *a pleasure-seeking person, eats twice a day*. "Tri bhuktam rogi," *sickness accompanies a person who eats thrice a day*. This ancient practice was substantiated scientifically by the biologist Yoshinori Ohsumi in 2016, who received a Nobel prize in Medicine for his research on fasting. He figured out that fasting activates autophagy, a Greek phrase that means "self-eating." According to Cleveland Clinic, "autophagy is your body's cellular recycling system." It helps the cell salvage the reusable parts and get rid of the junk. It also destroys pathogens like bacteria and viruses. As we age, this process slows down, slowing the rejuvenation of cells. Therefore, fasting gives the body the opportunity to activate this natural cleaning process, which leads to good health and longevity. Knowing the benefits of fasting, we should eat enough to nourish the body and not overeat.

An incident of dire hunger shook me to the core; since then, I fast every Tuesday. At that time, we lived in Calcutta, India. I was sitting in the car, and my mom had gone to the shop. I don't like to be in crowded places, so I convinced my mom to leave me in the car while she shopped. While sitting in the car, I was passively looking around, and this kid caught my attention. He was the skinniest kid I had seen, and he was eating food from the dumpster. When his eyes caught mine, he smiled and stood up; he limped and went off. He had polio in one of his legs.

I did not realize that I was crying, and tears were rolling down my cheeks. It was not that I had not seen poor kids begging at the traffic lights, but this was the first time I had witnessed the desperation of poverty and hunger. That evening, I related the incident to my dad and told him that it made me sad. He said that after all this crying and feeling sad, what am I going to do about this incident? I said, "to remember this day I will fast, and that way I will force myself to be hungry and never forget how blessed I am." From that day, I fast on Tuesdays and eat one meal in the evening. God has blessed me, for I can choose to be hungry, a luxury millions of people in this world don't have. They are hungry because they have no food or very little for that matter. Later on, in college, I joined the Rotaract club and chipped in a program called "Polio Plus" to prevent polio in babies. What this incident did to me was to do something about the thing that I did not like and to figure out how to chip in to make a difference, no matter how small. This is how I started practicing "Change worries to Concern!" We have discussed this phrase in the chapter "Healing through Praying". It means taking a step towards what we don't like and doing something about it instead of worrying and doing nothing. Now that I know that fasting is good for healing the body, it gives me added motivation to continue with this inculcated habit and discipline.

I was amazed to witness a scene in the Movie "I AM" directed by Tom Shydac. This experiment was conducted at the Heart Math research institute in California to show that how we eat matters. In this experiment, the bowl of yogurt, his food, is connected to electrodes with a meter that reads and records the reaction of the bacteria in the yogurt generated by Tom Shydac's thoughts. This is a visual demonstration to show that what we think when we eat matters for our health.

This made me think of an episode from my childhood that is an extension of the idea demonstrated by the above experiment. While cooking dinner, my mom accidentally burnt the vegetables, and my grandma told her that thinking affectionately about the people for whom we are cooking helps us not only avoid burning the food but also prepare delicious meals. Later on, when I started cooking and burning the food so many times, I understood what my grandma meant: to be present mentally in the action of cooking. This makes the process of cooking pleasurable and accident-proof.

To have a strong body, we need to exercise. It could be anything that speaks to us, like going to the gym, walking in nature, swimming, and practicing yoga. We need to choose and stick with it. My balance with exercise has come after trying various exercise regimens. I joined CrossFit for a while. During those days, I did not have the knowledge to exchange negative thoughts for good ones. To stop the parrot that was in my head from pushing me to the Negative Mental Energy State, I decided to join CrossFit. The exercise regimen was so difficult that while doing those workouts of the day, I had to be present with my mind and body in what I was doing. I realized that I could not sustain that rigorous exercise regimen without getting some kind of injury sooner or later. I come from a culture that is a big proponent of "madhyam marg;" *the middle path.* An extreme routine or regimen is very hard to maintain in a long-term goal. This mindset made me incorporate Yoga into my overall fitness regimen. I still do some CrossFit exercises, but they are toned-down versions that help me maintain my overall physical fitness. Yoga has now made me more connected to my body and mind without rigor and has provided a balance in my overall fitness regimen.

Taking care of the body is important for living a healthy and happy life. It demands disciplined and good lifestyle habits of hygiene, cleansing, eating healthy, sleeping, and exercise. **Health is wealth! This does not mean that good health is valuable, but it means that good health is priceless!**

Before you start reading the next section of this book, I want you to pause, reflect on what we have read, assimilate the relevant information, and evaluate it for your own energy management needs!

Let's ask ourselves:

1. What information mentioned in this section will enhance my energy and happiness?

2. Am I taking care of my body and mind?

3. Have I encountered setbacks and failures?

4. Am I healing?

5. What can I do to heal?

6. Is there any information or an activity mentioned in this section of the book that can help me to heal?

7. How can I develop my own coping mechanisms to my needs and heal?

SECTION 4:

Some philosophical questions for Energy Management

"The one who knows all the answers has not been asked all the questions."

Confucius.

Old Age and Death!

No matter how well we take care of our bodies, we will die. Death is "param Satya," a Sanskrit phrase that means "the ultimate truth." No one can dispute the fact that every being that is born will die one day. In this modern age, longevity has increased, but quality of life has decreased. It reminds me of the story of Tithonus from Greek mythology. Eos, Goddess of Dawn, fell in love with Tithonus and asked Zeus to make him immortal so they would be together forever. Zeus granted that boon. Tithonus ages to the point that he is withered and shriveled, but he cannot die. Lord Alfred Tennyson captures his pain and misery of everlasting life in his poem "Tithonus." In these lines, he depicts Tithonus yearning for death, and he is fed up with the gift of immortality.

…To hear me? Let me go take back thy gift:

Why should a man desire in any way

To vary from the kindly race of men

Or pass beyond the goal of ordinance

Where all should pause, as is most meet for all?...

Death like birth is a natural phenomenon and dying at a ripe old age is Mother Nature's gift to mankind. In modern times, life expectancy has increased globally. According to the United Nations, global life expectancy at birth for both sexes has improved from 46.5 years in 1950 to 71.7 years in 2022 and is expected to rise to 77.3 by 2050. This has made us live longer and work harder because we are worried about living in an expanded old age. Old age, in itself, is not a problem. Actually, it is great to be old, a privilege, but what makes us anxious is that unlike Tithonus, we are no prince with unlimited financial support.

If you are not familiar with the story of an ant and the cricket, then let me summarize it for you. The cricket enjoyed the summer singing and dancing while the ant collected food for the winter season. When winter came cricket had no food to eat while ant had enough to survive the winter season. This is a symbolic story where summer is our youth and winter is our old age. We are paranoid that we may turn like cricket in our old age with no food and no shelter. This paranoia makes us emulate the ant in the story, and we not only work in summer, the prime of our lives, but go on working.

We need to plan for our old age so we can enjoy the twilight years. We have to save and invest to enjoy these precious years of our lives with our friends and family. The problem is that no one knows when one is going to die and how the volatile market will play out with the financial investments for our retirement plans. The worrisome thought that we may outlive our savings makes us anxious. This anxiety comes from the unpredictability of the future. Not having a crystal ball to see the future has also contributed to making us a community of workaholics, and this is compromising our quality of life. Our life in this complex materialistic world is beautifully summed up by

William Henry Davis: "What is this life if full of care, we don't have time to stop and stare."

We all should save for old age and emergency situations and, while doing so, learn to pause and enjoy family, friends, and the gift of life itself. We can do so by being passionate about planning for our old age rather than being obsessed about it. There is a very fine line between passion and obsession. **Passion** comes from a place of positive thinking and progressive vision, and we are happy because while diligently working towards a goal that we have set for ourselves, we learn to pause and recharge by enjoying the simple pleasures of life. **Obsession** comes from a place of negative thinking due to fear and anxiety; we are unhappy because we are so focused on reaching the destination, and in doing so, we forget to enjoy the simple pleasures of life. Even though we are talking about passion and obsession in the context of financial planning and old age, this attitude holds true for life in general.

Old age is the time to give way to the new. Old age gives us the chance to sit down, relax, and enjoy the show. It relieves the pressure of being the lead actor in the drama of life. It is a beautiful opportunity to be an audience with the power to clap, an expression of showing our appreciation, encouragement, and support to the posterity. We need to have faith in the story writer, All-Pervasive Energy/God, who has written our unique stories with lessons and blessings!

To enjoy old age, we have to create our own "**Blue zone**." Blue zones are some places in the world where people live to a ripe old age of 80 and over, and they are happy too. The people living in these zones have a healthy lifestyle and a sense of purpose and belonging. Creating our "Tribe" and living an active, healthy, and meaningful lifestyle makes us "age like a fine wine!"

Knowing that we are all connected and that we are all part of the universal drama helps us live our lives with gratitude and purpose on this Mother Earth. When I got my yoga certification from a prestigious yoga institute in New Delhi, India, the gurus asked me to show them some asanas. They observe the correct execution with right breathing and mindful association with each asana. The next part of the test is philosophical questions that gurus ask. The head guru asked me, "How do you perceive God?"

I responded immediately, "Like mercury!" Everyone, including the guru, was puzzled. He asked me to explain. I said that when I was a kid, I saw the thermometer break and the mercury split into small droplets, but soon these droplets joined into one big ball of mercury drop! Later on, when I was in high school, while studying intermolecular forces, I came to know that mercury has a tendency to stick together because of the cohesive force between the mercury molecules.

I told the guru that I perceive God the same way. We all are part of one God or All-Pervasive Energy, and we are born on earth as God's part or droplets of energy. Therefore, we have a natural inclination to unify and bond with other droplets, God's creation. Wanting to connect is our cohesive force! We are born to serve a universal purpose. We are born to execute our universal purpose, and then we mingle with the All-Pervasive Energy or God! The gurus loved my answer, and they really liked the concrete example of mercury and the analogy.

Is death the end? No one really knows this answer. However, this is how I choose to answer this question. Just because we don't see far enough doesn't mean that something is not there. With our eyes, we can see to a certain distance, but with a telescope, we can see farther into the galaxy. Using the eyes as our best lens, we may have a limited viewpoint of the vast world. When we see the same world with a telescope, our vision and horizon of knowledge expand. **This means that "seeing is believing" depends on the lens that we use.**

When we follow a flying bird with binoculars, we can follow its flight to a certain distance. If we can't see the bird anymore, that doesn't mean that the bird stopped flying. The bird was already flying, and we were able to see just a portion of the flight with the power of the lens at hand. Thus, we did not see the beginning or the end of the flight. The human mind wants to perceive everything infinite, with a beginning and an end. **We are part of the infinite.**

With our finite knowledge, we know that the Big Bang happened about 13.8 billion years ago, and since then, the universe has been expanding infinitely. So, the point remains that this universe was born due to the Big Bang, but there was a parent that gave birth to this phenomenon. Therefore, the seed was always there, "**ajanma**," a Sanskrit word which means "cannot be born or is eternal" the big bang was the right nourishment for the eternal seed to express and grow itself as our universe. We want to understand our universe by making its vastness finite. We want to make everything linear, but the universe cannot be explained in a linear perspective; it is cyclic, and so is the cycle of life and death. We are products and part of the infinite, so we cannot be finite! Therefore, death is not the end!

No matter what perspective we want to choose about death, that is, whether our life here on Mother Earth is finite or we are part of infinite, death is inevitable, "param Satya"- absolute truth should encourage us to live with gratitude on Mother Earth and to our optimum potential.

We are born empty-handed and leave empty-handed. This means we do not bring any material possessions to this world and do not take any material possessions with us when we die. So, what do we actually take with us and leave behind? We take with us memories that we have built with loved ones, and we leave behind memories for them. My father-in-law passed on in 2022, and my dad passed on in 2024. The void is immense, but they live in my memory and memories of all those who love them.

Death is the celebration of how we live and what kind of memories we leave behind for the loved ones to hold on to.

When Great Trees Fall

By Maya Angelou

And when great souls die,

after a period peace blooms,

slowly and always irregularly.

Spaces fill with a kind of

soothing electric vibration.

Our senses, restored, never

to be the same, whisper to us.

They existed. They existed.

We can be. Be and be

better. For they existed.

Love is Multifaceted

Love gives meaning to life by adding value and fulfillment. It gives us purpose to become our best version as human beings. We generally think of love as feelings shared between two people. This is one aspect of love. Love has different forms; it is multifaceted. Love is a language of the Universe across species. The documentary on Netflix, *My Octopus Teacher,* is a great example that beckons us to widen our horizons to explore and understand love; however, before we do that, we need to differentiate between romance and love!

When we give or show love, we experience joy. However, we often confuse love with romance because that is what movies and media promote. It shows that people in love have excitement, thrill, and exhilaration in their lives. They are hugging, kissing, having sex, giving flowers, intimate dining, etc. We think this is love, and we want it in our lives so badly. I think it would be very exhausting to execute all the above throughout the day, all the time. It is humanly not possible because life demands commitment, responsibilities, devotion, and compromise, and these are basic qualifiers of love. Love makes us chug through the difficult or challenging times in our lives. Romance is a state of euphoria, and it is powered by excitement, thrill, and exhilaration.

It is always good to balance love with romance to spice up the relationships between couples. Let me give you an analogy: love is like staple food. In the USA, the staple food is bread, and just by eating bread, we can live, but adding lettuce, tomato, and other ingredients to make a sandwich makes that bread tastier. Love is like bread, essential for our existence. Romance is the extra stuff that goes on the bread to make it into a tasty sandwich.

Love grows between partners when we listen to each other, communicate and talk, argue and come to a consensus, laugh together, and just like each other's company. **Love fosters true friendship with commitment, care, and companionship!**

Love and romance both evoke desire between two partners. However, romance is limited to carnal, but desire, evoked by love, is not limited to bodily desires; it is the union of two souls. I understood the meaning of love between two people when my dad told me about an episode from the great Bedouin Arabian love story of Laila and Majnu. After Laila got married to another man, lovesick Majnu started loitering around with his broken heart and repeating the name of his love over and over again. One day, while he was walking in that state of desolation, he walked in front of a maulvi (priest) who was doing Namaz or praying. Maulvi got very annoyed at Majnu and said, "Are you blind? Can't you see I am praying?"

Majnu replied, "I am in love with a mere mortal, and I couldn't see you. How come you could see me while you are praying, which is a state of transcendental love?"

Love has different forms; it is multifaceted. Love can be a commitment to a cause. Jane Goodall's videos of her work and dedication to saving Chimpanzees is an example of love and devotion. Her observation that Chimpanzees make tools and use them for their own benefit busted the myth that only humans have the ability to use tools. Mother Teresa, the greatest humanitarian of modern times and a saint, indeed tended to those whom society has forsaken: the lepers, the destitute, and the orphans. **Her love was the love of service to the needy. Mother Teresa said that "true love is love that causes pain, that hurts and yet brings us joy."**

Love is devotion without ostentation! This story that I heard as a kid is an example of "bhakti," or devotion. There was a hunter who one day found a Shiv Linga in the forest and started offering meat to Shiv. He would hunt, roast the meat, and offer a portion to Shiv, then eat the rest of it. The gods asked Shiv why he was not upset because Shaivites bhaktas don't offer meat to him. Shiv said the hunter's devotion is pure, and he just loves him. The gods were not convinced, so Shiv said look at the Shiv Linga. When the third eye started bleeding, the hunter was absolutely distressed and said, "Shiv, your eye is bleeding. You just have one eye to see, but I have two. Don't worry; I will give you one of my eyes so that we both can see!" He pulled his dagger out to rip out his eye. Shiva intervened and blessed him. **The moral of the story is that love is unconditional devotion.**

Can a person who has suffered tremendous pain and suffering and injustice feel love and happiness? The Dalai Lama is a living answer to this question. He has gone through tremendous pain, suffering, and injustice in his life. He was uprooted from Tibet, his homeland, along with thousands of his fellow Tibetans, yet he loves everyone, and he is happy. He spreads love in the form of "ahimsa," nonviolence, compassion, and altruism.

Love is accepting and giving a chance to a fellow human being. There was a ruthless robber called Angulimaal. He used to rob people and cut off their little fingers as souvenirs and then wore them as a garland around his neck. One day, Buddha crossed his path. Angulimaal demanded to cut off Buddha's little finger. Buddha said to Angulimaal, "Cut off my little finger if that makes you happy." Angulimaal was puzzled to see a man who was unperturbed and tranquil in his presence; everyone he had robbed had feared him and asked for mercy. Buddha was offering his little finger without fear, with grace and serenity. For the first time, Angulimaal experienced true love and inclusion, not rejection. He was transformed in that moment, and he became a Buddha's disciple and lived by the principle of "ahimsa" or nonviolence! In this story, it is important to understand that Angulimaal was not born a robber; his circumstances made him become one. Buddha separated him from his circumstances and accepted him as a person.

I have witnessed the acceptance of a fellow human being without judgment! When I was little, I visited my ancestral village. One day, this man came asking for alms. My grandmother gave him a lot of grain and asked him not to steal. I asked my grandma why she said that. She told me that this man was a thief and that he was caught stealing. The thief told the village heads that he was stealing because he could not feed his children. Since then, the villagers have given him grain and food so he doesn't have to steal.

I asked my grandma, "Why do you give grains to the thief, and why did the villagers not report him to the police?"

She said, "No one chooses to be a thief; circumstances make them into a thief. Anyone will go to any lengths to feed their hungry children; the villagers understand that, and by giving him grain and food, they help him and take away his reason to steal!" This episode stayed with me, and it has helped me understand that love is kindness. Anyone can turn into a new leaf, provided he or she wants to change his or her situation and society understands. Kindness and forgiveness facilitate that metamorphosis.

We find love and happiness by sharing! My third-grade teacher told me a story about finding love and happiness by sharing! She said that heaven and hell are the exact replicas of each other; both places are beautiful and bountiful. When we die according to our karma, we go to heaven or hell. At the gate of heaven and hell, God ties a huge spoon on the hand so that we cannot bend our arms. Both heaven and hell have a huge banquet hall with the choicest food and wine. In heaven, everyone is happy and enjoys the beautiful place and people because in the dining hall, when they are seated across each other, they feed the person in front of them. Everyone eats well and enjoys God's heaven. In hell, at the dining table, everyone is trying to feed themselves, and the big spoon does not allow them to bend their arm and feed themselves, so they are hungry and cranky and can't enjoy the beauty around them, which is the same as heaven.

I am blessed to witness unadulterated, pure love all day long through raising Parag. Parag was nonverbal until age four, and now he can talk, but he is limited. We work on improving his functional verbal communication. However, I believe he communicates better than we do because he speaks in the language of love! He gives smiles, hugs, and kisses without holding them back. All these things are free, but we are still stingy about giving them freely. I notice that when people receive his loving smiles, kisses, and hugs, it makes them smile. Parag teaches me that love is infectious, and it is the most beautiful thing to spread in this world!

Balance is the Key to Happiness

We have heard the saying, "excess of everything is bad!" I believe a dearth of everything is bad too. When there is too much air, it is a storm, which can be devastating. Too little air means rarefied air, and we may have difficulty breathing, and we may die. Too much water means flood, which is disastrous, too little water means drought, and that too is detrimental. Too much food is gluttony and too little starvation. Balance is a point of optimum satisfaction. For example, when we eat a favorite candy, it is pleasurable but as we go hogging on it, the pleasure sensation decreases and then we may end up getting sick. This is the law of diminishing returns, a principle in economics. This point of optimization is neither less nor more; it is the point of balance, and at this point, we are happy and fulfilled.

Balance is the key to happiness! What does balance do? It takes away the conflict and centers us. We experience amazing synergizing of energy within and around us; this gives us a happy, fulfilling existence in this complex world.

Synergy happens when we are balanced in our thoughts, words, and deeds- the state of emotional equilibrium. That state gives us happiness and energy to deal with anything that comes our way. However, it feels impossible to be in a balanced state mentally, emotionally, physically, and spiritually. There is a constant pull from the centered state of existence. Only Buddha, the enlightened being, can remain in a constant balanced state and not react. They are like Noble Gases. The Noble gases are nonreactive because their outermost shell has eight electrons; they have full octet. Someway Buddha or enlightened beings' hearts are full of love and wisdom. Therefore, they too do not react under ordinary circumstances.

We are ordinary human beings, living in a complex world, reacting to a lot of stimuli. **How can we be balanced with ourselves? The answer lies in the "pause!** The pause is creating a space to reset! There are a set of unbalancing forces that work upon us. They are subjective depending on our circumstances. Let's understand "pause" and "restorative forces" with a visual example of a pendulum. Pendulum is at equilibrium when it is at rest, hanging straight down; only the restoring force of gravity is acting on it. When external force is applied upon it, then it moves back and forth, and the amplitude depends on the magnitude of the forces applied to it. The more force on the pendulum, the further away from the equilibrium or balanced state. Let's imagine we are the pendulum and then think about what forces are taking us away from our state of equilibrium or balance. The forces that imbalance us are mental, emotional, physical, and spiritual. We may be overwhelmed by our work, relationships, family issues, health, and spiritual void. These forces are kaleidoscopic, so they change with the change in situations. We need to evaluate them periodically. We must ask, why are we feeling this way? What will make us feel better? How can I achieve that?

To find the restorative force, the point of equilibrium, we need to pause, that is, create a space of introspection reflection and meditation, then recalibrate by responding and doing something concrete to reduce the imbalance.

When we become aware of these unbalancing forces, we want to get back into a balanced state as quickly as possible. So, we overzealously try to tackle all the forces that are off balancing us at one time, or we realize the multitude of unbalancing forces acting in our lives. We may want to do nothing about it because we think it is too late, that nothing can be done, and therefore, there is no point in trying. Both attitudes are skewed. One action is too much, and the other is nothing. Doing nothing is not the answer because nothing comes out of nothing. We cannot deal with all the off-centering forces at one time, but one at a time. Once we know each of these forces, then we need to deal with the most powerful force that is off-centering us. Kids with autism show deficiency in communication and socialization and demonstrate undesirable behaviors. Most of the time, parents and caregivers are bogged down and burnt out by dealing with undesirable behaviors. When we devise behavioral strategies for the most challenging behavior, reduce its intensity and frequency, and eventually extinguish it, we increase the quality of life of both the individual with autism and his caregiver. Tackling one force at a time helps us get nearer to equilibrium. The same strategy is applicable in life when we are off-centered. We need to deal with the most powerful off-centering force. These unbalancing forces could be work, family, relationships, and health (mental and physical). The next step is to figure out ways to make that force powerless by finding active solutions and acting upon it with consistency and disciplined practice. Gradually, we start calibrating back to our center occasionally, and with practice, we stay in that state longer.

How do we know that we are getting off-center to the point of meltdown? The ultimate response to sensory or emotional overload is a state of imbalance because there is way more on our plate than we can handle. The body starts to emit signals. The brain processes the external stimuli and transmits these signals as a warning through our body. We may feel a change in our breathing, heart rate, and body temperature, and our mood changes because of the stimuli. Then, we know that the situation at hand demands interception through some practices that help us avert breakdown through meltdown. Everyone must come up with their own practices or coping skills to intercept an onset of a meltdown, to create a space to recalibrate, and to the center without a breakdown.

When I feel a situation is making me uncentered, I do a couple of modified "Sitkari" breathing exercises. I put my teeth together, breathe in from my mouth, and release the breath from my nostrils. It has a great cooling down effect on the body and mind. Just conscious breathing through the nostrils and breathing out from our mouth helps redirect our attention to this action and helps us detach, which creates an intentional pause from the destabilizing forces. I also use perfume oil or "attar," which we have named Treasure Oil One, which Parag makes. It is a blend of orchid, orange essential oil, sandalwood oil, and almond oil. All these oils create a synergy that reduces stress and fatigue and enhances mental alertness. So, the result is body and mind working in harmony or balance. Aromatherapy helps us to center throughout the day. Research has proved that different scents have various effects on us. When we inhale these scents, the molecules travel from the olfactory nerve to the emotional center of the brain, the "amygdala," and make us feel a certain way.

To be centered all the time in this complex world is extremely hard. Pausing and creating a restorative force with introspection, reflection, and meditation gives us the tools to synergize and balance. We cannot be in a balanced state all the time, like Buddha, the enlightened being, because we are ordinary human beings. With practice, we can calibrate back to that state of physical, mental, emotional, and spiritual balance more often and for a longer period. **Heroism lies in practicing this extraordinary state of well-being!**

Epilogue

This book is a sincere effort to answer a question that has been asked recurrently by my audience in different ways. It sums up to- **How do you look so put together all the time despite the daily grind of dealing with Parag's autism?** The condensed answer to this question is in my first book, *"Autism Our Journey and Finding Happiness,"* in the chapter *"Parag's diagnosis and my cleansing."* This book is an elaborate answer to that question.

Being put together is generally associated with being well-dressed and groomed. We are the only animals in the animal kingdom who wear clothes. It evolved as a way to protect ourselves from the elements- heat and cold. Gradually, we evolved clothing into fashion, and being put together has become an expression of style and fashion. Dressing well and appropriately is important, but being put together in the real sense has to do more with the character that we build with resilience, tenacity, and fortitude. The dictionary meaning of put together is "to build, assemble and create." No matter how well dressed we are, if we are scattered internally in our mental and emotional state, then we are not put together in the real sense.

First of all, I am not put together and have patience all the time; only Buddha, an enlightened soul, is capable of that state of perpetual centeredness. I strive to be patient and not be scattered every single day of my life. Many times, I fail, but I don't stop trying because **when we love, we don't give in or give up**. If you think that, through this book, I make handling challenges in life look easy, then let me bust your bubble- **I know that challenges are package deals that come with life. Life is tough for everyone! Some of us have tougher ones.** So, what do we do, throw it away? Never! I shared that I am a self-taught cook, and I have figured out that when we have tough meat to cook, we use tenderizer to make it soft and tasty. The same goes for life; all the coping skills and hands-on, practical tips that I have shared are tenderizers to make our very tough life not so tough but rather enjoyable!

I run homeschool for Parag, and looking put together by being appropriately dressed is the requirement of the school decorum. "The school has a certain decorum. A dress code is one of them. Everyone dresses appropriately. When I am in pajamas, my brain goes into resting mode, and I am not alert and agile. School requires alertness of mind and body. During the early phases of the program, I realized that when teachers see me in pajamas, they too get lax; after all, the school is run at home. There is a dress code for every environment, and Parag needs to learn that as well. It would be ridiculous to see someone in a formal suit at the beach! (*Autism Our Journey and Finding Happiness;* chapter: School rules and decorum, page 138-139)."

Dressing appropriately stemmed from my need to be heard and taken seriously by the teachers who helped me run Parag's school. So, part of being put together is that I dress according to the occasion and give thought to it. Teaching Parag to be well-dressed and groomed has also stemmed from the need to protect him from infections, and it helps him to be accepted by his friends and the community. Of course, his charming personality helps as well. What we need to know is that one of the major causes of death not only for individuals with autism but for the special needs population is infection. This happens because of a lack of hygiene and grooming. We all know that "cleanliness is next to godliness". Making an effort to be well groomed and have a good hygiene regimen is a worthwhile effort to live a healthier life.

Being put together has a lot to do with not being scattered like a headless chicken. Moving through the day with purpose is a huge part of being put together! As a mother and a teacher of a son with autism, I have to always be ready to turn a bad day into a good day and a good day into a very good day. Shedding emotional baggage before entering Parag's classroom to teach has been a pretty hard practice. In the beginning to turn off a mental switch and turn on another one without any perforation was not easy. This compartmentalization or being present at that moment for the work at hand has come with practice. I have shared these disciplines and practices in this book. The day I know I am off-centered and cannot regroup, I choose not to teach Parag. I make up for that day when I am aligned with myself. When we are unaligned in our emotional state, then our thoughts, words, and actions are not synchronized, and it creates discrepancy rather than harmony. **Working in synergy is a huge part of being put together.** This allows us to perform and deliver our best work in whatever we choose to do!

I did not know I had so much patience until it got tested! To be put together demands patience from us! In raising a kid with classic autism, tantrums and meltdowns are a part of life, and it demands herculean patience from the caregivers. I have patience because I get tested for it almost every day of my life, and most of the days I win now because I have developed coping skills and knowledge to deal with these behaviors better. Parag has developed coping skills along with communication skills to deal with these behaviors for himself. Anyone will get better at anything when they get tested for that, and they don't give up.

Our attitude gives us the energy to persist. Our attitude determines whether we will sustain the pressure or not. When our attitude is anchored in positive thinking, it oscillates between the high mental energy state of joy and the low positive mental energy state of happiness. It prevents us from sliding into the negative mental energy state of hopelessness. **Once we start resonating in a positive mental state, we automatically start the pathway for emotional well-being. We are put together internally, in mind, body, and spirit, and we become whole again!**

What makes us believe "we can" in the darkest of moments? Hope! Hope is not regulated by logic but by blind love! In my talks, I say, "Hope is the only dope that we should take twenty-four seven." When we are **hopelessly hopeful,** then everything in the universe synergizes and gives direction to walk the walk and talk the talk. Tenacity comes from believing and pushing through with determination, even when the whole world thinks it is impossible. Prayers help heal and replenish hope! Praying has helped me to get rid of my "why me" phase. Praying is a huge comfort, and it renews my energy to live life meaningfully with grace!

This incident helped me to understand the value of "practicing what you preach!" My dad and my sister went to listen to Shri, Shri Ravi Shankar, the founder of "The Art of Living!" After listening to him, my sister tells my dad, "Whatever he said, I already know!" My dad said, "The difference between you and him is that he practices what he preaches. You just know but do not practice; that is why he is the renowned yogi, and you are not." When my sister told us this story, we were young. We laughed, but I understood the depth of my dad's concise statement.

In this book, I have shared the practices, principles, values, and coping mechanisms that I have accumulated over the years and have been practicing. I still slip and falter, but the stories, anecdotes, and coping skills have been like a mnemonic device, helping me to retrieve and retain relevant information in time of need and help me get back on my feet faster with renewed energy and enthusiasm.

I hope and pray that this book," *Energy Management Mantras for Caregivers,*" helps you to manage your personal energy better. In taking care of our energy- physical, mental, emotional, and spiritual- we become better caregivers because energy keeps us going with enthusiasm and positivity. Life is kaleidoscopic, always changing and creating new possibilities of opportunities for growth, learning, and happiness! I have written this book, *"Energy Management Mantras for Caregivers,"* with humility and a pure intention to help. **Through this journey, I throw the seeds of Love, Courage, and Hope into the Universe and wish them grow and multiply!**

Namaste- I bow to the Divine in you!

"To strive, to seek, to find, and not to yield."

Lord Alfred Tennyson.

This is the last section of this book. I want you to pause, reflect on what we have read, assimilate the relevant information, and evaluate it for your own energy management needs!

Let's ask ourselves:

1. What information mentioned in this section will enhance my energy and happiness?
2. Old age and death are inevitable- how am I choosing to live?
3. How can I find love and happiness?
4. How can I create balance in my life? What "restorative forces" do I need to activate?
5. Life is tough: what coping skills should I develop for my needs, to live a healthy and happy life full of energy and enthusiasm?

The Author

Mamta Jha Mishra

Mamta Mishra was born in India. She earned her master's in English literature from Delhi University of India and her master's in special education from Jacksonville University, Alabama, U.S.A. Certificate of completion Harvard Business School Core Curriculum, Diploma in Computer information system, Certification in Yoga, and Certificate in cosmetology.

Mamta lives in Gadsden, Alabama, with her husband, Dr. Pranav Mishra, and two sons, Ankur and Parag. She has published a book, **Autism: Our Journey and Finding Happiness.** It compiles 25 years of the journey in dealing with Autism through her son Parag. Mamta is an entrepreneur; she has started an online venture **https://paragcosmetic.com/**to help Parag excel in his vocation of making Ayurvedic cosmetics! The vision through this venture is to incorporate more special needs individuals and help them in their "pursuit of happiness!" and financial independence.

Through the Autism Foundation of Gadsden, Alabama, she started an annual Autism Conference called "Together We Can Make A Difference" in Gadsden, Alabama. Her vision is to share this conference on a digital platform all over the world. She is bringing Autism Awareness and acceptance through talks, TV interviews, and a Facebook blog.

Apart from being a dedicated mother and a teacher, she also loves to do organic gardening, yoga, and CrossFit. She has run two marathons: The Seven Bridges Marathon in Chattanooga, Tennessee, and The Utah Valley Marathon in Provo, Utah, as well as a few half marathons.

You can contact the author at mamtajhamishra.com, email her at mamtamishrabook@gmail.com, or message her Facebook page, Autism Our Journey and Finding Happiness.

References:

Scherer, K. 2009. The dynamic architecture of emotion: evidence for the component process model. Cogn. Emot. 23:1307–51. doi:10.1080/02699930902928969

Article: "The Sustainable Happiness Model and Pie Chart: A Heuristic Framework for Understanding the Influences on Well-Being"

Bernstein, E. (2014, October 6). *How You Make Decisions Says a Lot About How Happy You Are*. Wall Street Journal. **https://www.wsj.com/articles/how-you-make-decisions-says-a-lot-about-how-happy-you-are-1412614997**

Britannica Dictionary

Daniel E. Stanton, Jackelyn Huallpa Chávez, Luis Villegas, Francisco Villasante, Juan Armesto, Lars O. Hedin, Henry Horn

Epiphytes improve host plant water use by microenvironment modification.

- Fisher HE, et al. (2015). Four broad temperament dimensions: Description, convergent validation correlations, and comparison with the Big Five. https://www.frontiersin.org/articles/10.3389/fpsyg.2015.01098/full

Goodreads. (n.d.). *Barry Schwartz (Author of the paradox of choice) Quotes*. Retrieved January 6, 2021, from **https://www.goodreads.com/author/quotes/6957.Barry_Schwartz**

https://bio.libretexts.org/Bookshelves/Human_Biology/Book%3A_Human_Biology_(Wakim_and_Grewal)/10%3A_Introduction_to_the_Human_Body/10.2%3A_Organization_of_the_Body

https://courses.lumenlearning.com/wm-biology1/chapter/reading-the-second-law-of-thermodynamics/

https://en.wikipedia.org/wiki/%C4%80%C5%9Brama_(stage)#:

https://ibcces.org/blog/2019/04/04/special-needs-travel-fastest-growing-segment-of-the-market/

https://my.clevelandclinic.org/

https://pubs.acs.org/

https://www.authenticityassociates.com/emotions-are-energy/

https://www.bluezones.com/2018/10/fasting-for-health-and-longevity-nobel-prize-winning-research

https://www.britannica.com/science/history-of-medicine/Traditional-medicine

https://www.healthline.com/health/largest-organs-in-the-body#largest-organ

https://www.hopkinsmedicine.org/health/wellness-and-prevention/ayurveda

https://www.nytimes.com/2016/10/04/science/yoshinori-ohsumi-nobel-prize-medicine.html

https://www.poetryfoundation.org/poems/45389/tithonus

https://www.theodysseyonline.com/strive-albert-einsteins-mother

Oxford Dictionary

Paradise Lost by John Milton,

When Great Trees Fall by Maya Angelou

Ulysses by Lord Alfred Tennyson

www.ingramcontent.com/pod-product-compliance
Lightning Source LLC
Chambersburg PA
CBHW072234270326
41930CB00010B/2122